T0354803

Better Than This

an inspiring true story of
grit and finding one's destiny.

WRITTEN BY MARK HOLIS

Balboa Press books may be ordered through booksellers or by contacting:

Balboa Press
A Division of Hay House
1663 Liberty Drive
Bloomington, IN 47403
www.balboapress.com
1 (877) 407-4847

Print information available on the last page.

ISBN: 978-1-5043-9256-3 (sc)
ISBN: 978-1-5043-9257-0 (e)

Library of Congress Control Number: 2017918532

Balboa Press rev. date: 05/03/2018

"Just because you're eating out of garbage cans,
doesn't mean that you are garbage."
– M. Holis.

This is a true story

A VERY RAW, REAL,
And emotional story

WHAT STARTED OFF AS MY PERSONAL JOURNAL in which I wrote in every night before I went to bed and every morning when I woke up, has now become the book that you are holding in your hands.

What you are about to read are the stories of my life and those who reminded me just how astonishing life can be, at a time when I believed that I was without value, isolated, depressed, and contemplating killing myself.

While reading this you will come across personalities and events that have shaped me to become who I am today. Some good. Some bad.

To honor them, and the stories I am about to share, the names, locations, dates, and personalities have been changed to respect their privacy and integrity.

What you are about to read is an inspiring true story of grit, finding one's destiny, through the good, the bad, and through starvation. Be forewarned, outside what my publisher would allow, nothing has been held back.

Fasten your seatbelts and enjoy every word…for this is my life.

TABLE OF CONTENTS

'Better Than This'

An inspiring true story of grit and finding one's destiny
Plus; 7 steps to getting out of any situation fast!

DEAR ME, I LOVE YOU
A letter

DEAR ME, I LOVE YOU

A letter to myself

FOR THE FIRST TIME EVER, I absolutely believe that I am in love... with myself.

This is not an egotistical thing but a true realization of who I am and who I'm not. I've accepted the fact that I am not perfect, that I have my flaws, and that my flaws, as perfect as they are will cause others look down on me, talk bad about me, and I am fine with that. If you looked down on me or chose not to be a part of my life, then you weren't meant to be a part of it, and that itself is a blessing. I also know that if it wasn't for my flaws (as perfect as they are) that I would not be who I was meant to be. I would not be who I am today. I am not meant for everyone and I get that, but for those whom I am meant for, it is an honor to be in their lives as they are in mine. This is not an egotistical thing, but a true realization of who I am and who I'm not. For the first time ever, I acknowledge and write this to myself: *Dear Me, I Love You.*

Happily, ever after,
Me

CHAPTER ONE
I Want to Cry

CHAPTER ONE
I Want to Cry

THE FOLLOWING SENTENCE IS BY FAR, the hardest I've ever had to write in my entire life.

It has now been one week since I've been homeless.

I have one bag, two shirts, one pair of pants, and one pair of socks. I've been surviving for the past week on just five dollars a day for lunch, dinner, and breakfast. Now, if you are doing the math, (and trust me, I am) you'll notice that five dollars a day split between three meals per day is just $1.66 per meal. This doesn't include paying tax. These five dollars a day is in the form of rolled up nickels, dimes, and (if I found a few laying on the ground that day) quarters. Change that you discard, accidentally drop on the ground and ignore, because it's just pointless to you, is what has become priceless to me. Why? It's what I have been using to eat—your loose change you otherwise deem useless. You know the penny that happens to fall on the ground and because you decide is too much work to bend over and pick up?

Yeah, that penny. With a collection of other pennies that I've accumulated for the day, hopefully they will add up to the $1.66 I need to get a meal tonight. I do not have any paper currency at all, not one single dollar to my name. I don't even know what I did with my wallet, but I tell store clerks, "I can give you a dollar in rolled up pennies if you take that." I've found myself asking that a lot lately. "Can I give you a dollar in rolled up pennies?" Hoping and praying that he or she would say "yes". The rumble in my stomach is so loud, I can barely hear myself speak, and I can barely hear their answers.

"How did I get here?" Is another question I find myself repeating, but I can't think about that right now. Right now, I need to eat something, before this hunger takes control of me, and eat something fast.

(Journal break)

Just two months ago I was living in a decent two-bedroom condo in a less desirable part of town, complete with wall-to-wall carpet, gated community, modern appliances, social clubhouse, a gym, pool, a jacuzzi, and 24-hour security. I had standards, and I had my likes in life. These were some of the things that I refused to live without. Can you believe that I would complain when I would go looking for apartments and they didn't have those amenities? I also had a beautiful woman (as a partner and friend) and I had a beautiful nine-month-old son whom I had the pleasure of waking up to every day. I remember being there for the delivery, changing his diaper, feeding him, and teaching him how to walk. I loved and still love those moments. I also had a bed…

As I catch myself reminiscing, it's almost funny. Yeah, I actually had a bed. I had a car; which I shared with my ex, but it was really hers. At one point, we had three, but I had lost mine due to falling behind on the car note. That was the beginning of starting to lose everything. I also had a job that paid the bills. I was managing a call center and making $650 a week. I complained about that too. Just like anyone else, I thought I was underpaid and barked at anyone who would listen about how I needed more.

Today? Well, today I have nothing. No bed, no car, no life partner, no son, no job. Absolutely nothing. Today, I'm lonely. Today, to survive I'm searching for food in someone else's garbage.

I catch myself reminiscing. At this point it's really all I have. It helps keep my mind off that fact that I'm eventually going to be eating something out of a dumpster that will be covered with ants. I reminisce about my old job and how much I hated the fact that I barely had money. There seemed to never be enough money after bills, diapers, and rent. I thought constantly, "How can anyone live like this?" I remember being pissed about only making $650 a week, and I mean *pissed.* Now that I have no idea of what or when I will be eating again, I only now recognize that $650 a week was a blessing. Not only was it a blessing but I took it for granted and I fucked it all, royally. Today, $650 a week to me would feel like having the keys to the bakery and eating all the chocolate cake inside in one sitting. It's not just the $650 a week salary that I should have appreciated, I should have appreciated my life and I didn't appreciate that for shit. I was infatuated with owning as many material things as possible and living way above my means. I was too busy wishing that I had someone else's clothes, someone else's lifestyle, someone else's money. All too busy not appreciating what I had, continually looking over the fence for greener grass, for a greener pasture. Not contempt with myself and what I had, I was too busy to notice that I was about to be blindsided.

Today, I couldn't give two shits about what someone else is wearing, what someone else is driving. After I found myself stripped of every little thing I had, I finally realized that I had everything I needed. Today, I have absolutely nothing except this sandwich which someone has already taken three bites out of. Nothing says "loser" like looking for dinner in someone else's garbage can.

I've never been so lonely, so cold or so hungry. So, now that I'm collecting change on the ground to eat something that isn't covered in ants, what do I do? There must be something better than this.

(Journal break)
The introduction of Eric.

It has been months since becoming homeless and today is the first day of interviews. I finally have something positive to write about in my journal, for the first time in a long time. If it wasn't for my new best friend, my only friend, Eric, I have no idea where I'd be. Who is Eric? Eric, believe it or not, is my old boss. We had linked up after I had called him and told him what was going on. That I decided that I wanted out of this. That I had hit rock bottom and I begged for his help. To my amazement, he obliged.

I worked for him in the call center that he owned a very long time ago. I started working for Eric as a phone agent, quickly rose through the ranks to supervisor, assistant manager, and finally manager. Nine months later, the call center ended up closing because by the time Eric took it over from the old owner, the company was already hemorrhaging $150,000 (if not more) a month. After closing his call center, we stayed in touch and became friends in the process. Today, if it was not for that friendship, I would be sleeping under a bridge or in a dumpster instead of in his office. After I became homeless, Eric offered up his office (or, to be correct, "office suite") for me to sleep in until I got back on my feet.

This suite was in a building with a bunch of other little office suites and for the most part, was small. Just sixteen by fourteen feet. There aren't any windows, just a box with four walls, a few broken computers, and a buffet-style table that was used as a desk. There is one thing good about this small office suite, though. Not only is there a door and my own sense of security now, but there's also a working computer, and it has internet access!

Now, I don't have to tell you how much of a blessing this is. I now have access to the outside world. I can create a resume, look for odd jobs on Craigslist for quick cash, and set up interviews. That's exactly what I do in exactly that order. Mind you, I still must survive on five bucks a day of loose change, without a car, one outfit, and no way to take a shower or shave. At this point I had a fully-grown beard on my face, so getting a job is going to be somewhat of a challenge, but having the internet is a damn good start. I'm optimistic for the first time in a long while. I am grateful for Eric and what he's done for me beyond belief. More than he will ever know.

After just a few days in his office creating a resume and submitting them to job postings on Craigslist, I get lucky. I've spent countless hours online putting in my application and sending my resume to every place or kind of job imaginable. Clean toilets? Not a problem. Sell oranges on the side of the road? I'm not above that. Sweep out a warehouse? Can I start tomorrow? I've lined up a few potential job opportunities doing just about anything anyone would hire me for. Today, in other words, is interview day! I don't have any interview clothes and haven't showered in forever. As a matter of fact, I'm sure I smell horrible, but I'm not letting that stop me. I'm going to get out of this.

Up until I start to feel the weight of the outside world crashing in and the thoughts of failure returning. They hit me like a ton of bricks. Just like that, I lose my optimism. The conversation in my head quickly begins to change. Questions in my head arise, *can you have fallen any further, you fucking loser? Begging on Craigslist to clean other people's toilets for $7.25 an hour? You used to hang out with people who drove high-end exotic cars and now look at you...You're worthless.*

I shake my head aggressively from left to right to get those thoughts out of my head. I can't think about that now, it will only lead me down a road of depression and nothing ever gets accomplished by being depressed. I've got to think forwardly, plan my next step and make a move. I need to think positively. After all, I have the internet, a friend, a resume, and fortunately, a roof over my head. I can do this.

Yeah, I'm still sleeping on the floor, but I've got these four walls. I've got potential jobs starting to call me back with employers who are interested in interviewing me and I know it's not much, but finally, I also have a glimmer of hope.

So, fuck you, voice in my head. I'm not going to play your games anymore.

CHAPTER TWO
Rebirth

CHAPTER TWO
Rebirth

MY NEXT THOUGHT IS, *how am I going to get to these interviews?* and *If Eric can do it, please God, make sure he isn't busy today. I can really use a ride and I really need this.*

I pick up my phone, hands clammy from the nervousness and call Eric. Would you believe, thank God, Eric is available and has agreed to take me? And I have three interviews today. Somebody upstairs must still love me. Next hurdle? Trying my damnedest to look hire-able, to get presentable.

I have two halfway decent shirts and one pair of 'passable' interview quality pants, so finding something to wear to these interviews won't be that hard, considering that I only have one outfit. The problem isn't the outfit, though. The problem is that they're dirty, they stink (they haven't been washed since I've been homeless) and I essentially look like a bum. I haven't used mouthwash in forever and my hair hasn't been cut, either. I remember when I used to get it cut every Sunday. I treated it like a chore. I thought, at the time, that it was tiresome to get in the car and take the ride to the barber to get my haircut every week.

Today, I dream about getting my haircut again. I haven't showered in forever and my beard is now fully-grown in.

Unkempt, it's thick, raspy, and can easily be confused as a bird's nest.

Living in Eric's old office suite is a blessing at this point because I do have a roof over my head. I don't have to worry about my shoes being stolen while I sleep, and I'm protected by the outdoor elements. However, being without the necessities like shower and clean clothes, and being without a place to call "home", is starting to really take its toll on me. I miss home, I miss the little things. I miss having a kitchen, a refrigerator, and if I had any food, a place to store it. I miss cabinets, a living room, my favorite TV shows, a couch, a bed, a bathroom, shower, mirrors, a toilet, and clothing that don't stink.

There is a bathroom here. It's the type of bathroom where only one person can go at any given time, and there is only one for all the people in this building. If I had to guess, there are about 200 business suites here. To get presentable, I must head to the public bathroom to wash under my armpits, in between my legs, and to do what I can do to "freshen up" before my interviews today. I hope that none of the men that work here will need to use the bathroom while I'm getting ready. If they do, they will have a long wait on their hands.

Now, keep this in mind: the office suite that I am living in is not in the nicest part of town and the type of people that hang around this place are, as some would say, are unsavory.

You can guess the kind of characters and what kind of "activities" that these characters could bring with them while they're hanging around this building, which, I might add again for emphasis, is on the wrong side of town, and if you don't get the picture yet, is infested with criminals. These 'characters' I will get into later.

Back to the bathrooms. By the looks of them, you quickly realize that the bathrooms here sometimes are used as a haven to shoot up or get high in.

They are disgusting, to say the least. But I have a key, so I head to the public bathroom with my key in hand to freshen up. To brush my teeth, to try to wash my armpits and private parts with the hand-washing lotion that can be found in the wall dispenser. Never mind, the type of paper towel here. It's the kind that cuts like paper if you try to dry yourself the wrong direction. This is where having a towel, a private bathroom, and shower would come in handy. I get to the bathroom. Thank God, it's not occupied and there's no one inside shooting up. I know because I can see the green "unoccupied" sign on the door is showing. There is a green sign when the bathroom is not in use and a red sign reading "occupied" when it is. I use my key to gain access and lock the door behind me. The last thing I need are the neighborhood addicts busting in to use the bathroom as I'm washing my private parts.

After locking the door behind me, I make my way to the toilet. I place my washcloth on top of the toilet, a washcloth which I "borrowed" from a hotel, and I use this opportunity to see what I look like in the mirror.

As you can imagine, just like this bathroom, this is no ordinary mirror. The only reason you would call this a mirror is because of where it is placed: above the sink. This "mirror" is made of metal, not glass, but shaped like a mirror, with a somewhat reflective component to it. This mirror is where I also do my positive affirmations.

Being positive is something that doesn't come easy anymore. Since going homeless, it's something that I've been trying to do a lot of to help me put myself outside of the current situation. My affirmations have a double purpose for me. Not only do they keep my hopes up, they also help my mind busy. With my toothbrush and washcloth on top of the toilet, I stare in the mirror and start my affirmations.

"You're going to get hired today. You are going to get a job today! You're going to get through this! You're going to get back on your feet. You are going to have an address that you can call home again! You will no longer be homeless! You're going to get your son back and you are definitely not a loser."

These affirmations have become a religion for me because they help me remain positive in a time where I have nothing to be positive about. Plus, I refuse to be in this position any longer than I must be. I'm going to get out of this. I keep telling myself.

After I finish my affirmations, I start the process of getting ready. I reach over and grab my washcloth from the top of the toilet. Not fully paying attention, I grab it and lift up. The wash cloth unrolls, and time begins to slow down. Time slows because as I watch my towel continue to unroll, I completely forget that my toothbrush is inside. I knowing what is coming next. My washcloth completely unrolls, and like a fucking idiot, my toothbrush falls straight into the toilet. Seconds pass like hours. Looking down into the toilet, staring at my toothbrush floating in the bowl, I realize that the only thing I had in this world that connected me to my past life, the only thing that I was holding onto —my hopes of getting my old life back, my dreams, what once reminded me that I was once human, that I was once a man— is now floating in the center of this toilet. It's over now.

I have been stripped of absolutely everything now. My son, my house, my car, my job, my dignity and now at this point, mentally, I've had it. I'm fucking done. I completely break down. I lose it. Now, and only now, at this point I realize that I've completely lost everything. I am officially broken. I cry, uncontrollably. I clasp my hands to my face. My knees give way, and with my back against the wall (ironically), I fall to the floor. I cry like I've never cried before. This moment is so surreal. It's not because it's just a toothbrush or my last toothbrush. It's because of everything that toothbrush symbolized. I've had that toothbrush forever. I had that toothbrush when I had friends, a job, an income, my son, a girlfriend, bills, a car, responsibilities, a home. When I was human. And now it's gone, all of it. What you see as a simple toothbrush...I see me and my life. Floating in the toilet.

After the tears have dried up and after what feels like hours, I get up. I realize where I am. I don't mean in a public bathroom, I mean in life. I am a fucking loser. I realize with crystal clear vision that this is not where I was supposed to be in life. That I am not a loser, that I am a real person, with real human emotions. I realize the day I have ahead of me, the interviews, the promise, the opportunity, that any one of these jobs can turn my life around at any moment. I decide in this moment that I will *fight!* I decide that this isn't my life! That I am a fighter! That I will turn this whole thing around! I will win! That I will succeed! I stand up, refreshed, reinvigorated, and reborn.

Standing up firmly, I walk over to that toilet, I look down, and I see my toothbrush, a.k.a. my life, floating in the center. I immediately plunge my fist into the center of it and pull my toothbrush out. I hold my toothbrush high in the air and in the loudest roar I have I shout, "This is *my* toothbrush! You will *not* take this from me. *Fuck you*, life! *Fuck you, toilet!" FUUUCCKKKK YOOUUUUU!*

I rinse my toothbrush off. I clean it with the same hand lotion I use to wash my private parts with. Once I get all the soap out of my toothbrush, I put toothpaste on it and brush my teeth like there's no tomorrow. I brush them like a fucking champ. I swear my teeth are getting whiter and whiter by the second!

I start to repeat, "I will *never* be beaten again, this is my *life* and I will *win!"* I own this moment. I feel a new life has just begun and that I have officially left all excuses and my old life behind. I fucked up —yes, I get that—but, you will not have this. The past is yours, but the future is mine!

Quintessentially in this same exact moment, I feel as if I am in an open field with nothing but possibility and freedom in front of me. In this moment, I feel reborn. I feel renewed… I feel…

I pick my head up and look directly into the mirror. I drop my chin, with my chest out, I firmly say, with all belief and anger that I have inside of me, at the same time with such positivity for the future and the new me.

"Fuck you and fuck this. Welcome to the rebirth of M. Holis bitches."

CHAPTER THREE
I'm on fire

CHAPTER THREE
I'm on fire

I HAVE BEEN HITTING THE JOB SITES and postings on every job-related website imaginable hard lately. I live in Las Vegas, and the unemployment rate is currently at 14.5%. Go figure. After my mental breakdown (or as I would like to call it, a breakthrough) I've noticed that I've gotten lucky lately, because not only was I able to send out my resume to a good handful of jobs, but I've been able to line up four interviews today as a result *and* Eric, my new and only friend in the world, is available today and is willing to drive me to them all! *Thank you, Lord, this is amazing.* Who knows, there just might be a way out of eating out of garbage cans and being homeless after all!

And, if you can believe this, on my way back from the bathroom, my boss before Eric calls me out of nowhere. He told me that he has an old paycheck for me. A commission check that they've had for quite some time and that I never picked up and obviously never cashed. I mean, can you believe this?

"What is going on right now?" I say this with extreme happiness and a smile on my face from ear to ear. Not only has it never been picked up or cashed, but they have it waiting for me! I had to ask, "How much is it?"

My old boss says, "Sixty dollars."

I reply, "Sixty dollars! Are you kidding me? Where are you? I'll pick it up right now! I'll be there in two and a half seconds!"

I'm sure they *never* had anyone so ecstatic about picking up a $60.00 paycheck before in the entire existence of their business. I'm probably still talked about around the water cooler today about my reaction, but what can I say, God is good. This is an incredible opportunity to get back on my feet.

My old boss tells me, "I'm on the strip about to eat right now. Why don't you come by and pick it up? I'll be here for a little while." Of course, I agree and soon after we hang up, I immediately call Eric.

I can't seem to dial his number fast enough. My fingers are pushing all the wrong buttons and numbers. I'm so excited. I finally get his number typed in and his line starts ringing. He picks up.

Eric asks, "Sup?"

I prattle in my excitement, "I know that you have already agreed to give me a ride to my four interviews today and I totally appreciate it but, please, please tell me that you are available like, right now?"

Eric answers, "Not really, but why, what's up?"

"My old boss before you just called me and told me he has a check for me. That one of my old clients called up and placed an order about a month ago and that they have a commission check waiting for me with my name on it!" I explain.

"Oh, that's huge! How much is it?"

I exclaim, "Sixty bucks!"

For a moment, there's silence. He finally says, "OH, well, sixty bucks is good."

I know that he was just trying to be polite. He knows that sixty bucks isn't shit, and I know that too, but who gives a fuck. Sixty bucks in cold hard cash might as well be six million to me right now!

I ask, "Well? Can you come by the office now? He's on the strip eating and I have to get over there before he's finished."

Eric agrees. "Sure. Give me fifteen."

I gasp, "Man, you are too awesome. Thank you so much, bro!"

"No prob. I'll be there in a bit."

We hang up and I can't believe how excited I am. I feel like I've just won the lottery. I feel like I want to do something, like I want to go run a mile in record time! I want to jump through these walls and over this building.

My excitement is immediately crushed when I look down on the ground and see my clothes. They are wrapped up and currently being used as a pillow. My crusty socks are lying next to them. Crusty meaning, they haven't been washed since I've been homeless and as you can guess, they smell like it too. I am reminded once again of the fact that I am homeless and that this will be the first interaction with anyone, besides Eric, who knew me prior to the life I'm living now.

He's going to see me and immediately recognize the fact that I am homeless just by my clothes. If he doesn't, he'll know by the first time he gets a whiff of me. If he even recognizes me at all. Fuck me.

I look around as if the New Clothes Fairy just happened to magically drop off a pile of brand new clean clothes in a corner somewhere without me noticing. My phone rings. It's Eric. I answer. He says, "I'm here." I hang up. Yep, I'm officially leaving this office to meet my old boss. This is going to be interesting. More like a complete embarrassment. I leave the office, hop in Eric's truck, and we head down to the strip. It's not long before we get there.

I call my old boss (we'll call him 'Dwayne') to see if he can have someone come down and bring me my check so that I do not have to see him.

Dwayne answers. "Yo! Where are you at?" "I'm here,"

I say. "Hey, can you have someone bring the check down to me? I'm double parked and my friend doesn't want to get towed."

Dwayne scoffs. "Are you kidding, bring your ass up here! I haven't seen you in forever. Don't be a bitch!" As if that's all I must worry about. I should have known this wasn't going to be that easy.

I protest, "But like I said, we're double parked ---"

Dwayne cuts me off. "Bro, get your ass up here!" He hangs up.

I look down at my phone and wait five seconds, hoping that he would call me back, having changed his mind and wanting to send someone down to deliver my check. No luck there. I turn to Eric.

I sigh, "Looks like we're going up."

Eric frowns. "There? And you…"

I know what he wants to say: "Me? Walk in public with you? And you, looking the way, you look?" But he didn't, because he is a friend. I respect him for not saying anything.

I nod. "Yep, I need that check."

Eric hesitantly agrees. "Okay then, if that's what you need, then let's go get it."

He could have easily said that he'll stay in the car and wait as I go get it, but he didn't. He's coming with me and that by itself is the essence of what friends are for. One for all and all for one.

We get out of his car and head up the escalator on the strip, then up the stairs to the restaurant where my old boss is. Again, this is the first time I'm in a public place looking and smelling the way that I do. I can feel the looks, the stares starting to happen. The whispers as I walk by people creeping up. I imagine them saying, "Oh my, do you smell that?" and "Stay away from him, kids," but, I have one thing on my mind and that's getting that check. It is easy for me to pass them by and miss the looks the host and waitress give me as I make my way into the restaurant. I pass them like I own the place, trying not to make eye contact.

As soon as I pass them and make my way into the downstairs dining area, I get a text from Dwayne. "I'm upstairs eating outside on the patio," it reads. Geez, you mean I must walk past even more people smelling the way I do? This check isn't coming easily. I finally make my way upstairs and find him, just like he said, eating along the balcony overlooking the strip. I see him, he sees me, and we make eye contact.

When his eyes catch mine, they go from, "There he is!" to "There's no way that's him," in just a flinch. It's as if the closer I got, the more his eyes were saying, "Please turn around. I do not know you," as if he wished in that moment that I would keep walking and spare him the embarrassment. Keep on walking and save him from having to acknowledge that he knows me, at least in public. With my own agenda in mind, I ignore the signs to keep walking and I get to him.

I greet him. "What's up, bro? What's going on?"

Dwayne has a look on his face like he can't believe what he's seeing. "Um? Nothing. Are you okay?" He doesn't hesitate, he asks, "What's wrong with you? Are you hungry?"

I only shrug. "Yeah, no I'm fine, I'm good. Just going through something right now."

With my check in his right hand, Dwayne very, very slowly, because he's still in shock, gives me my check. I can tell that he still can't believe what he is looking at. He says, with serious concern in his voice, "No, seriously. Dude, what's wrong with you? Are you okay?"

Trying to make me feel a little bit better about how direct his questions are he asks, "Do you want a beer?"

I reply, "No. I really can't. I have to be somewhere, but I really do appreciate it!"

Dwayne stares. "Um, okay, man? Well get better…or something."

I don't know what that is supposed to mean, but I say, "Thanks." I point at the check. "Thanks again man, I mean it."

Dwayne nods. "Sure…"

I give him one last head nod of thanks. I turn my back to catch Eric standing a good ten feet away from me. I get it, I probably would have done the same thing, I guess. Stand just far enough away where no one would know that we're there together, but close enough to say that we slightly know each other. I turn and walk away, and Eric and I head back downstairs, out past the host stand and out the front door.

Well, that was demeaning and sucked, I think to myself. The walk to the truck was a long one, but as we stepped closer and closer to it, my heart started to beat just a little bit faster.

The experience I just exchanged with Dwayne seemed to dissipate with every step closer that I got to Eric's truck. Why? Because I have a check in my hand and I know that the next step is cashing it! I can't wait to get in Eric's truck to open it, to see the amount and make sure my name is on it.

So exciting! We get to his truck. I hop right in and rip open the envelope. My name is on it, yes! The amount is $60.00 and it's made out to cash. Fuck yeah! Totally making everything I just went through completely worth it. I'm freakin' ecstatic right now!

Eric asks, "So what now?"

I answer happily, "Check cashing store, fucking food, and then the second-hand store."

"I get check, cashing, and fucking food, but the second-hand store?"

I explain, still excited, "Yeah, for really cheap used clothes. I've got interviews today that I have to get to and after all, I got to look the part."

Eric agrees. "Okay! Let's do it!"

I'm getting a job today. I can feel it!

So, Eric and I take off. We head to the check cashing store, then the dollar store and then the second-hand clothing store. With my new-found glory (cash money in my hand) we get myself some used interview clothes. Nothing major, but enough to pass the first initial test when getting a new job, looks and the smell of your clothes.

Currently in my backpack I have one pair of pants, socks, shoes, boxers, and two shirts. I've also been wearing the same clothes day in and day out. I've been sleeping on the floor in them for months now without a shower. Not only do I smell funky but, without having access to a washing machine or a shower, I'm sure that my clothing smells like it too. We arrive at the bargain store. I head to the men's section and quickly begin to go through clothing that was donated by other men who are clearly living a better life than I am right now.

Carefully I go through donated shirts, pants, and socks while trying to stay within budget and get the cheapest stuff possible. The idea here is to get an entire outfit that I can feel proud of and feel good in. That means "look" and "feel" the part. So, I'm going through all kinds of clothing, locating by price, then eliminating the ones with rips, stains, and/or tears. I've got enough of those already in my backpack. Finally! I find something. I find a few things. I run to the changing room with my new-found treasure to make sure they fit. It's been so long since I've tried on clothes.

I've pulled size 36 pants which used to be my size when I was healthy and had a bed to sleep on but, they fall right off my waist. Down past my knees and hit the floor. I've lost a lot of weight and in this moment, with or without a mirror, I can tell why Dwayne told me to "get better." I come back out and Eric and I start going through the men's clothing again, this time for much smaller shirts and waist sizes. This time we pull size 34 pants and Eric grabs a pair of pants off the rack, holds them up high and says, "Do you like these?" Poor Eric, he thinks I'm shopping for looks.

To appease him I say, "Sure."

Eric warns, "They're a size thirty."

"I'll grab them anyways," I say.

We both return to the changing area with clothing now that I hope will fit me. I try on the size 34 pants. They do the same as the size 36s, fall straight to the floor. I try on the size 30s for shits and giggles, and they fit. Unbelievable. It's now that I realize how much being homeless has taken its toll on me physically. I can only imagine what it's doing to me internally. The good news is that I have new clothes, I have a few bucks in my pocket, literally, and that means options. I pull my emotions out of the gutter. *"Everything fits!"* I yell out loud. I bolt out of the changing room area and run to the checkout, and I do mean run! It feels as if the clothing had an expiration timer on them and if I didn't get to the counter on time they would disintegrate. She rings me up. "Forty dollars, please." Cha-ching!

Now, I know what you're thinking. I've been surviving on rolled up nickels, just got paid sixty bucks, and I just spent eighty percent of it on buying second- hand clothes? Yes! Remember, I don't have a stove in Eric's homeless man's charity office and I can stretch $20 a long way at the dollar store. So, we leave the second-hand clothing store with two pairs of pants, a sweater, a dress shirt, two pairs of socks, a new pair of dress shoes, and a new hat. I had to get the hat. It's the only way to cover my hair which has been obviously neglected.

Everything matches and is interchangeable, so I basically walked out with something like five outfits for the price of two. I walk out of that store feeling as if I *am back* for the first time today! This is a great moment and I just want to baste in it, if only for a moment. With some change leftover, Eric and I hit up the dollar store for my "life start over/make over kit" and for food that doesn't have to be wiped clean of ants prior to eating.

Arriving at the dollar store, I pick up one pair of nail clippers, one razor, one shaving cream, one brand new toothbrush (I'm sure you knew that was coming), toothpaste, underarm deodorant, and mouthwash. I throw them in the cart. Now, it's time for food. Ahh, food! I get three loaves of bread, two jars of peanut butter, two jars of jelly, and one gallon of water. Fifteen dollars spent. Whoo hoo! I don't spend the entire twenty. I keep five bucks in my pocket because I haven't had any solid dollar bills in my pocket for months. These five dollars represents more than just money: It represents hope. A belief that with a little bit of money in your back pocket and some luck that even a homeless man can take on the world. I have everything that I can ask for. I have the basics. I have food, shelter (even though it's on the floor in Eric's 14 x 16 windowless office suite), and clothing. So, I keep it, the whole five bucks, in my back pocket all to myself. We check out and leave the dollar store. What time is it? Crap! We've got to get back! I've got to get ready for my interviews, pronto!

Eric drops me off at the office building. I thank him a gazillion times, say goodbye and I get out. Right before the door has a chance to bang close behind me, I look up. I just so happen to notice a barber shop on the second floor of the building I'm sleeping in. How did I not notice this before? Is it possible with a few bucks and a little bit of hope in your back pocket that your eyes open that much wider than they did before? I don't know. What I do know is that my mind is

too busy coming up with ways of getting my hands on an electric razor to shave this bird's nest off my face and head.

Now, I only have five bucks and I don't intend on spending it, not for nothing! But, here's the plan. The plan is to go up there, ask them if I can borrow one of their electric hair cutters so I can get rid of this "rat's nest" called a beard off my face and get my hair cut or at least shave it down to something manageable.

I eagerly run upstairs, walk in their door, and everyone, and I mean the one customer getting his haircut at ten in the morning and the two other guys that resemble barbers. I immediately turn their attention to the door and stare at me as I enter. The guy to my left resembling something of a barber says, "sup?" giving me immediate permission to approach him. At least in my head that's what it means.

I walk up to him. I ask, "Do you work here?"

He says, "Yeah, what's up?"

At this point my voice drops down to a whisper, kind of like a secret mission is about to take place because I do not want anyone else to overhear what I'm about to ask him. "Do you have a pair of hair clippers I can borrow? I need to take this bird's nest off my face for a job interview I have today."

He eagerly replies, "I can take that off for you!"

I stammer, "No, you don't understand. I can't pay you to take it off my face for me. I don't have any money." In an even deeper voice I whisper, "I'm homeless. I don't have any money and I really need this right now. I have four job interviews today. I promise to bring them right back to you *or* I can shave it off right here. It doesn't matter to me."

Time stops. He pauses to think.

I recognize this moment. It's the same moment I had in the bathroom when I dropped my toothbrush in the public toilet. Nothing is said for about thirty seconds. He tilts his head to the right and looks at me with a strange look as to say, "Are you crazy or something?" but nothing is coming out. Nothing is said.

The "crazy look" in his eyes seems to slowly dissipate. His head returns to its regular position and he says, "Ok...fine." I swear I could have kissed him. But, he's a big black man and I'm sure he would not have appreciated it, so I ignored the idea of kissing him on the cheek. He says, "Where are you going to cut your hair and shave your beard off at? Are you in this building and if so, what unit are you in?"

I say, overly excited like a kid in a candy store, "I'm in 135!"

He says, "If you're not back in five minutes, I'm coming downstairs for my clippers and to fuck you up!"

I say, "No problem!"

The weird "crazy look" returns to his eyes again as if he thought that his big black ass coming down to my unit to kick my frail little ass for not returning his clippers would be somewhat be enjoyed by me. Another look comes over his face but, this time it's not the look of crazy.

Anyhow, he digs down into his barber drawer and pulls out a pair of nice hair clippers. He doesn't give these to me. He puts them in his left hand, digs down again and pulls out another pair of clippers. Those aren't bad either. He doesn't give these to me either. As a matter of fact, he doesn't even look at me. He then goes down for a third time, pulls out a third pair of clippers. He looks at them, looks at me, and says, "Here, you can use these."

He hands them to me and I immediately know why he was looking so hard. They literally were the shittiest pair of hair clippers known to man! They look like they were originally purchased in 1906. Like he gave Jesus his first fade with these. But I don't care, nor do I mind. I know he didn't have to say yes and for that alone I am truly grateful. He looks at me as if to say, "Well, are you going to take them or not?"

I do, and I dart down to the public bathroom on a mission with the big black man's hair clippers and my new second-hand clothes.

Bathroom's available? Yes! Time to get busy!

I enter the bathroom, lock the door behind me, find an outlet, and go to town on my face. I can only assume what it might have sounded like outside that bathroom. Just imagine, the bathroom door is locked. You hear a mechanical buzzing sound coming from behind it and a man obviously happy with himself screaming, "Oh, yeah! Oh my gosh, this feels so good!" You know what I'm talking about. You get the picture. I don't care, though. In record time, I cut off the bird's nest beard from my face. Save myself about ten years. Darting out of that bathroom, I head back up the stairs into the barber shop, skipping my hair cut with time to spare. I walk up to that same barber, out of breath as I hand him his clippers.

He looks at me and says, "Who the fuck is you?"

This time I reply with a look of my own as to say, "Superman!" Instead, I say, "Thanks." I turn my back to exit and dart out of the barbershop door and back down the stairs. I still need to get clean shaven, but dollar store kit" and head back to the public bathroom for a those clippers saved me a bunch of time. I head back down to the little office suite I've been sleeping in. I grab my "life start over/makeover second time. This time I head back for what my ex would call in my days prior to going homeless, my "getting pretty" time.

I shave the rest of my beard off. I cut my fingernails for the first time in months, toenails (which now resembled talons), wash my face, under my armpits, and man business.

I finish up, take one look in the shiny metal mirror, and proudly say to myself, in all my glory, with a smile on my face, "Well Mr. Holis, you sure clean up nicely...for a homeless guy."

CHAPTER FOUR
Are you fucking kidding me?

CHAPTER FOUR
Are you fucking kidding me?

I EXIT THE PUBLIC BATHROOM AND HEAD BACK TO THE OFFICE. Time to get ready for today's interviews. The tiny no window office where I have been sleeping on the floor has never looked so cramped after receiving such positive news and hope so far today.

Time to throw on my brand new (well they're not brand new, but they are to me) second-hand clothes and try to look as presentable as possible for my interviews today. They are all lined up one after another, starting in the next hour. I put on my hand-me-down pants, my second-hand button-down, my slightly worn sweater, my hand-me-down hat, and just as I'm putting on my hand-me-down sneakers...
Trust me, some of you cannot go the entire week wearing the same thing twice. Can you imagine having to wear the same clothes you are wearing right now and not being able to take them off for the next four months? I bet you can't. So, when someone throws you a pair of second-hand pants, you're

going to treat them fuckers like a gosh damn $320 pair of Versace jeans. My phone goes off, (how is this thing still on after not paying the bill for four months? I have no idea) it must be Eric.
Yep! It is. No need to answer. I know he's calling to let me know that he's outside. I tuck in my shirt that I bought at the consignment store and grab my journal to document the day and I'm off. I exit the building and see Eric.

I hop in his truck, thank him for the rides to the interviews today and we begin to bullshit. Just to make it easier on Eric, I mapped out all my interviews and set them up back to back on purpose. I set them up so that the first and the fourth interviews today are both close to the office. The second and third are the farthest interviews from the office. I did this so that we basically, after all four of my interviews today, we would have driven in a continuous circle, instead of shooting from one side of town to the other like five times without direction and wasting his gas in the process. It wasn't long before we get to my first interview. I'm nervous. Many thoughts are running through my head at this point. "Please, I hope that I do not smell?", "Please give me this job", "What if they can tell that I'm homeless?" and "I hope I make the right impression", "I hope that I'm not underdressed", "What if they ask me about not bringing a resume?", "What if they ask me about wearing a hat to an interview?"

How am I supposed to answer these questions? I can't really answer, "Well, you see, I have absolutely no money to pay Kinko's to print out copies of my resume or any money to go get a haircut because it's been four months now since I've been homeless. My hair is out of control and obviously, I wouldn't have copies of my resume either."

I snap back to reality and finally realize that I need to build up the courage to exit Eric's truck and get to this interview. You know what? No matter what they say, it can't hurt any more than losing everything you've ever worked hard for. Nothing hurts more than being ignored and being homeless. I open the passenger side door, get out, close it behind me, and make my way to their building. I can't help but feel like I have this walk that seems to be exhibiting confidence. I can feel it. I feel like a million bucks even though I know that I don't look like it.

I find their suite, I take one deep breath, I exhale, open the door, take one step inside and there it is. "Are you fucking kidding me? *FUCK!*" Two problems: one, I've seen this before. I can tell by the cliché framed posters on the walls of inspirational pictures with quotes underneath them, saying things like "Teamwork; together we achieve" and the best one "Ambition: the journey of a thousand miles… blah, blah, blah." That this is a typical MLM (multi-level marketing) or Vegas fly–by-night company that just opened its doors. Did I mention the telltale sign? Massive hiring. The lobby is filled with at least twelve applicants all waiting their turn to interview, and probably all for the same position, ultimately. If I wasn't in the position I am in I would have turned tail and ran as far away as possible, but damn, I need this job, whatever it is. And guess what? As if I didn't have enough worries, problem number two: are you kidding me?

All the people being interviewed for the position are all wearing expensive-ass fucking suits! As I sit here in my worn out second hand clothes, argh. Well, there goes making a good first impression. This is not going to be fun.

The receptionist calls me over just as I finish entering and asks me who I'm there to see. I mention the interviewer's name and she suddenly gets this shocked look on her face, as if to say, "Oh, you're here for an interview?" She takes a moment to look me up and down and then looks me straight in the eye, as if she was waiting for me to scream "Gotcha!"
Are you fucking kidding me?

But the "gotcha" never comes and she finally gives up and hands me an application. No words are exchanged. OH, this sucks. I take my application, sit down and try my best to act "business like" while apparently being underdressed. After sitting down, I cross my legs, sit up proper and fill out my application with such attention that from afar, you would've thought that I was writing the next speech worthy of a Nobel Peace Prize. Then the unimaginable happens.

As I brought my legs up to my knees to cross them I catch a whiff of my socks that I have been wearing every day for the past four months. Yes, the smell is coming through my shoes." These are the same socks that haven't been washed in four months. I uncross my legs and place my feet back on the floor. Oh my god, they smell so horrendous! And, just my luck, it just so happens that the girl sitting next to me, who is also here for an interview, is a totally fuckin' hot.

At this point I just want to roll up in a ball and die. With nothing else to do, I try my best to hide the smell of my socks and wait.

Interviewee number three gets called, then four, nine and so on. I'm number thirteen and I know I'm going to be called shortly. Sweat starts to build up under my armpits. "No! You can't do this to me now!" Obviously, I have no deodorant on. When's the last time you had a shower? I thought I cleaned my arm pits in the public bathroom this morning. I just know that if I sweat any more than I already have that I will smell even worse than my socks, I'm sure of it. "Quick! Think of something to take your mind off being nervous and sweating!" Oh wait, look, my nails are filthy, perfect! I look around for a business card, corner of a brochure, anything that can be folded in half to clean out my fingernails with. Anything to get my mind off being nervous. Ah, notepads, perfect!

I take the sheet, fold it in half twice and begin to "secretly" clean out my fingernails (Ah, the things we take for granted, particularly nail clippers) thinking I'm getting away with murder. I clean out my pointer finger on my left hand, and then thumb and as I'm starting to work on my other fingernails, I look up.

The fucking receptionist is staring at me as if to say, "Is it not enough you came dressed to an interview like a dirt bag? Now you have the nerve to start cleaning out your fingernails while waiting for your interview?"" People have no idea how mean they can be with just one look alone. Now she starts slowly cursing me out with her eyes.
I look back with a really mean look of my own as to say, "Yes, bitch! I am cleaning out the dirt from underneath my nails with this piece of paper while I'm waiting for my interview and you know what? I'm starving, I'm homeless, I'm desperate and yes, I'm pissed at the world so leave me be." Oh, she's a feisty one, because it doesn't work. Next, we begin a stare- down contest.

Her eyes slowly leave mine and turn to the floor then slowly back to her desk and onto her desktop computer. Did she get tired of staring? Did she feel bad for me and let me win? Who cares! I win! Ha! was my first thought. No awards here, no blue ribbon, no trophies, just a tiny window, a moment into my soul that lets me know I still got it! The ability to win! I don't care if it's a girl, I won! My next thought? Thanks to her, I'm going to kill this interview, not because I deserve it but because I now have the confidence to do so. Not to mention, I know it will kill her to have to see me every day from this point on from nine to five, Monday through Friday and every time that she sees me she will know that I'm the guy who she lost the stare-down competition to, oh yeah, it's on!

Number ten is called, number eleven is called, and number twelve. I'm next. My fingers are cleaned, and my interviewer comes out and yells "Number 13."

I raise my hand and say, "That's me." Just proud enough to get the snobby receptionist's attention and to give her one last look of my own before I get hired!

Of course, my interviewer is a 'dressed-to-the-T.' Young guy, 23 or so, so he doesn't give me a look of disrespect, even though he can, and even though I'm sure he's thinking what everyone else is thinking: This is how you came dressed to your interview? I can almost hear him saying it, but again, he doesn't say one word. Even though he could have, and he hasn't, in my eye that makes him a good guy. Thanks guy, I appreciate it, I say to him in my head. We make our way past what seems to be a call center bullpen, but there's a few things missing. Where are the people? The cubicles? The chairs? Ringing phones lines? Computers? Okay, boiler room anyone? Vegas is infamous for these kinds of operations. This should be fun. He leads me to his office.

Decorated and built to make an impression, obviously. Nice new glass desk. Nice new black high-backed leather chairs. This would make anyone still in college or recent college grad with not much "real world" experience very happy to be in a situation where they are being interviewed with this guy and this company, but not me.
This company and the whole process is starting to get under my skin because I am not in the position to be wasting my time. I could have used this interview time to interview with a legitimate company somewhere else. You know, the typical forty-hours-a-week job with a real paycheck at the end of

the week. I know this is going to be commission or MLM only. I know it, I can feel it. Not to mention I probably just wasted Eric's time.

I start to notice the little things that speak louder than his leather loafers. Nice desk, but there is no computer. No pictures of his girlfriend, or boyfriend, you never know these days. No pictures of his family. No typical wall clocks of London, New York City, Texas, and California time zones. These are things that you would find in a legitimate office job. None of the typical "I measure my existence with frivolous awards that remind me that I am somebody" stuff posted up anywhere. Hmm, this must be a temporary office for this guy, that's if this is his desk and office at all. Yep! I prepare for the worst. We start talking about my past work gets to how he founded the company. Finally, he talks about the job and the typical lame old boring interview structure and process. When I owned my own company, I asked "out of the box" questions and stuff like, "Is there anything you would not do for $300 million dollars, if you experience, he talks about himself, finally would not have to harm a stranger, yourself or anyone you know?" Simple, unexpected questions designed to bring the truth out of the person being interviewed and give me an understanding of their personality type, and of who they were, personally. This interview on the other hand, is not unique at all.

Then he hits me with it. "Now, the position pays commission only. Are you okay with that?"

I pause before I answer. Now, I know what you're thinking., "You're homeless, you're sleeping on the floor in your ex–boss' tiny office, and a man offers you a job, even if it's commission only, *take it!*" No, I did not. You're forgetting that I have a son I must get back to and support, and this does not happen on a commission-only job. Also, I could care less about the commission scale. Without a car, a shower, nice clothes, and money to get out there to meet people to sell whatever their product is, I'm screwed. I politely decline, I tell him about my situation, leaving out the fact that I've been homeless now for four months.

He swiftly and politely thanks me for coming in and gets up to as if to say, "This meeting is now over," and to walk me out of his makeshift office. Our interview was all of 3 minutes. The good news? Well, for someone else it's not a boiler room type business at all, it's just another commission-only position with a company with a lackluster product, no real system in place and hype and steam for sales. Regarding my interviewer, I still like him for not saying anything to me or giving me looks for being underdressed for my interview. I assume he just recognized much faster than others that I must be going through some shit. He was a Gent. He's going to make some girl happy one day.

I make my way past the empty call center "bullpen", past the other makeshift offices and out to the lobby. The receptionist and I catch eyes one more time, but she gets no love from me. I quickly picture myself as the Wicked Witch of the West in the *Wizard of Oz*, saying as I exit the lobby door, "We shall meet again one day, my pretty," (Insert evil laugh). I make my way out to Eric's truck. I finally let out a long sigh. Nothing these days come easy. Oh well, I sigh again, hopefully the next job interview won't be so taxing on me. Hopefully the next job interview pays...something.

CHAPTER FIVE
Maybe I should get boobs?

CHAPTER FIVE
Maybe I should get boobs?

I'M STARTING TO BECOME VERY, VERY ANNOYED. I feel like I won't be able to find a job today. After leaving job interview number one, where everybody was fucking wearing expensive ass fucking suits, my outlook for the rest of the day, I must admit, has been tarnished. Interviews number two and three were just as bad, if not more of the same as interview number one. Interview number two was with a call center that sold long distance phone service to businesses that was paying by commission only and to add a personal note, a fucking joke. Interview number three was just as bad as the first two, and with Las Vegas suffering from a 14% unemployment rate, everything that I've been interviewing for has been a joke and finding quality work is going to be harder than I thought.

No time to think negative, there must be a reason why Eric was available to give me rides today to my interviews. There must be a reason why I've been able to get as many interviews as I did today so, from this point on we're only looking up and forward!

Interview number two by the way: I'm interviewed by this kid who claimed to be the owner of this new company that is supposedly going to change the world and call center world at the same time. To start off, this kid was 10. Seriously, there was *no* way he was one day over 21, I would be floored if he came out and said that he was 30, absolutely floored. He had this trendy five-o'clock shadow thing going on, but it didn't work for him because the hair on his face seemed to have grown in sparing patches. His face looked like he woke up this morning and collected all the facial hair his dad had shaved off in the bathroom and glued it onto his face to look older. Seriously, he looked that young. Not to say that someone who is 14-, 19-, or even 21-year-olds can't change the world. Obviously, they can, but what I'm getting to is that everything this kid was saying and how he was acting did not match up to what I saw in his office. If you talk a big game, you should at least be able to dress a big game. Meaning, your shoe, and outfit game should be on point. To give you an idea of what I mean by 'The message doesn't match the messenger' Let's start with what he is wearing.

First off, have you ever heard of the word 'Fugazi?' If you have, then you will know what I mean when I say that he's wearing 'Fugazi' diamonds in both ears. Nothing wrong with that, but he swore up and down that they were real. This was only complimented by his amazing gold chain that, by the way, when the right amount of light hit it at just the perfect angle, would show you its true color, which was green. Oh, and did I mention how his green——I mean gold chain was incredibly gaudy and amazingly horrendous? As we would say in Jersey, he's a clown and he's loud. He walked and talked like New York City swag, but he wasn't born with that kind of "swag", even though he tries really, hard to pretend he was. As a matter of fact, before I walked into his office I overheard him on the phone with the Arizona Department of Motor Vehicles. Mr. CEO was arguing with them and trying to get his license back! Good for him, but his call with the DMV was on speaker phone and the volume was loud, and I mean all the way up! To the point where you can hear his conversation from down the hall. He demanded, "Fuck you, put me on the phone with your supervisor." The girl on the phone replied, "Sir, I don't have to take this kind of verbal abuse from you." If he treats the girl at the DMV this way over the phone, I can only imagine how he will treat me once I start working for him.

This is completely unprofessional, especially if you are expecting interviewees to come in at any given moment to interview for a position with you. He notices me standing there and invites me in and motions his boy out of his office, as if to say, "Handle that for me." His boy leaves the room, but leaves the door open so I can now overhear his boy on the phone with the DMV, and now his boy arguing with them back and forth. Great first impression, right? What an amazing day so far. So, the interview begins. He immediately begins talking 'at me' in the interview, telling me all about himself and how I'm going to make a million dollars working for him here. He tells me about his product. Best thing since sliced bread and how he landed this amazing office that, by the way, is run down and just a stone's throw away from one of many 'suspicious' and dirty low brow strip clubs here in Vegas. The kind of places where you catch an STD just driving past the place from the outside. "Liquid lunches anyone?" I imagine something being yelled every day at noon by the floor supervisor. He suggests that we take a walk around his 'office' and see the call center for what it is.

We make our way out of his office and take a quick right, then we walk ten feet and here we are, in his 'call center'. Once again, same as the first interview, there aren't any phones. There aren't any desks, and where are the people? There aren't any. I'm confused. Don't you need people to qualify as a 'call center'?

He says, "Imagine this being all yours as a manager here at my call center." I'm sorry, do you mean this 11x12 space with banquet tables set up as makeshift desks and PCs dating back to the nineteenth century? I immediately get the feeling that I am being transported back to the office that I'm sleeping in. Without any people to man them, I can't wait.

At this point, I've had enough. After all, I have Eric outside waiting for me. I need to get to my next interview and I don't have the time to entertain this guy, so I politely cut him off. I tell him that this opportunity is not for me, and without saying any other words, I make my way out of his office. Don't get me wrong, I do have an imagination, I can create things without needing much money to do it with and I have managed call centers (legitimate ones) in the past, but this guy had no idea what he is doing and no idea how he is going to do it.

He has no idea of how many people he will be hurting with his lies and false promises. Not to mention, I'm looking for a guaranteed paycheck every Friday, not an 'opportunity'. I'm looking for money I can rely on to get my life back, I'm looking for a definite way out! And this was certainly not it.

The following interview, interview number three of the day, was a mixture of both interviews one and two, total crap. Again, total waste of time and commission only.

What is going on in this city? Doesn't anyone want to pay for true talent anymore? Well, let me rephrase that, because in Vegas there is never a shortage of men who are willing to pay young women for their 'talent' who are 'dancing their way through college.' What I meant was, outside of strip clubs, are there any employers that are willing to pay men (and women) with true office talent anything anymore? I wonder if they would be willing to pay me if I got boob implants. Sorry, random thought. Anyway, the final interview of the day, and the only glimmering hope I must try to make this day productive, seems to be good, but I've said the same thing about the other three right before those interviews. I'll cross my fingers.

Once again, it's back into Eric's truck and off to the next interview. We head to the final job interview of the day. This interview is with a moving company that brokers out their moving jobs to moving companies, trucks and drivers. Since they do not have any of their own day laborers, trucks or drivers, they just facilitate moves and sell those moves to other moving companies that could use the business. I can only assume, just like the rest of my interviews today that this job could, or will be, commission only and most definitely a complete disappointment. Beaten mentally, emotionally and just plain tired, we get to the final interview of the day. Here we go again.

At first, I'm taken back. This building, as well as the other buildings in the complex, are nice looking. They're brand new, two-story corporate buildings in the nice part of town, with decent restaurants within walking distance and nice cars in the parking lot. Not that this means anything, but it's a lot better than where I've been and what I've seen so far today. I think I just saw an electric Tesla. Okay! My fear of, 'This interview will be a complete waste of time,' is starting to dissipate. I'm starting to feel like I'm in the right place for the first time today, and I'm starting to grow a little bit more confident, and should I say nervous, about this interview.

I exit Eric's truck, asking him to wish me luck, for the fourth and hopefully last time today. I make my way to the building and head up two flights of stairs. I take a right and I'm walking down a hallway with suite-sized doors. It reminds me of where I'm sleeping now. I make my way down the hall, counting down the suite numbers until I find them, 'Number three-sixty-six, three-sixty-five, ah, there's suite three-sixty-four.' I get there, but before I knock on the door I noticed that the door is cracked. I place my ear up to the door. I hear voices, like real voices of real people, on real phones, probably sitting at real desks! Finally, a legit job offering, but lets not get too excited now. Thinking this must be their suite, without hesitation, I walk right in. I walk in and to my surprise? Oh my God! First off, there aren't thirty fucking people waiting in the lobby for the same fucking job with expensive ass suits on! Jackpot!

Secondly, I walk right into their call center and everyone is dressed casually. Not like business casual, like polo's and dress pants but casually, like jeans and sneakers! *Thank you, God! Whoa!* I'm going to fit in perfectly here with my two pairs of pants and one shirt to my homeless self. Oh gosh, I'm starting to get excited. Not to mention they have a decent sized office, and as I look around I see all the computers are brand new, and people who are on calls! Not only that but the chairs are brand new, the desks are brand new and the phone system is brand new! Hell, I can even smell the fresh paint on the walls and did I mention, *there are* phones here and people calling on them! Imagine that! The buzz from the conversations happening over the phones here are contagious and fantastic.

As I stand in awe, I hear a voice come up from behind me and he asks questionably, "Are you Holis?"

What? You know my name and you didn't call me Number thirteen? I like this place already. I turn to see a thin, confident, middle aged European man. Very well kept and like I said, confident. I reply with, "Yes."

He says, "Welcome!" He has a genuine smile on his face, I might add. He then points to the office in the back of the room and says, "Follow me!"

Let's call my interviewer Justin. I follow him through the call center floor and to an office in the back corner. The entire office, including his, was not spared when it came to expenses. Brand new desk, brand new chairs, brand new monitor, pictures of his family in brand new picture frames (yes, he had pictures of his family in his office), wall clocks representing the time in London, New York City, and California, and even the smell of freshly painted walls seem to flow into this room. Interview number one today from my day today should visit this guy's office and take notes.

He points at a new office chair in front of his desk and gestures for me to sit. I happily take a seat. He begins to tell me about what they do here, what makes them special, and then he looks down and picks up my resume. As he does so, I look over and notice my resume is the only resume on his desk. Last interview of the day? The only interview for the day? Who knows. But I like his style. No one likes to come into an interview and see the interviewer dig through and pull their resume out of a stack of ninety resumes, just to hear the interviewer finally say, without any energy, "Oh, here you are."

I always hated that, it's bad interviewing techniques by the interviewer and starts the interview off on the wrong foot, because now the one being interviewed has no incentive to sell themselves when they know that they are one out of ninety others that you must go through.

When I interviewed potentials for the companies I worked for I never ever had any other resumes on my desk other than the person I was expecting to be in my office at their scheduled time. I wanted them to know I cared about them, that I was not just going through the motions, and that their interview mattered. I would like to think, for the most part, the interviewee took notice and performed that way. My interviewer, Justin, does the same and I already respect him for it. He begins to look over my resume and says, "I'm impressed." If he knew I was homeless, I don't think he would be so impressed. We chat and talk about my experiences and I hold nothing back, except for the fact that I'm homeless. I explain how I ran call centers, and always try to perform at 135% of my best. He cuts me off. I think, *oh crap, I said something wrong or said too much. Over-embellished perhaps? Gosh, control your nerves.*

He pauses, and then says, “I want to hire you. When can you start?”

This is one of those moments where the earth stands still. Like when I dropped my toothbrush in the toilet and when I asked the barber for a pair of hair clippers. It’s that kind of moment. I must have been silent for what felt like minutes. I can’t believe that I have a job. I almost reached over and kissed the man. *I can’t believe that I have a job.* It takes everything I have not to break down and cry. They would be tears of joy, obviously. I keep it together. Finally, I have a job. *I have income.*

I say, “Yes, Absolutely!”

This look comes over his He says, with a look of concern, “But you have no idea what the job pays.”

Did he just say “pay”?

He immediately, with a slight hesitation, goes into explaining what the pay is and how it is paid. I can hear the gulp in his throat. “The job pays 8.75 an hour.” He pauses and then goes silent. He has this look on his face as if to say, *I know this could be an insult to you with the experience that you have so…if you want to slap me, you can!*

I without hesitation say, with a huge smile on my face,” No, I’m serious. I’ll take it!”

His look changes from concern to joy, like he was thinking, did *he just say yes? He’ll take $8.75 an hour?*

Hey, you must start somewhere, and this is my starting point. Yeah, it’s $8.75 an hour. Yeah, it’s slightly over minimum wage but it’s a way out of being homeless! It’s a startface as if to say, “Really?” He can’t believe I said yes. The look disappears and then he says, “Great! You’re hired! Be here Tuesday morning and make sure you’re ready to go!”

We exit out of his office. Me personally, I want to high five every person I see on my way out as we cross over the call center floor. Like, ‘Guess who just got a job? Me, that's right! Guess who's going to be here on Tuesday ready to go? Me, that's who! Fuck yeah, bitches!'

I left that interview feeling amazing. I haven't felt like this in my four months since going homeless. It feels good. I feel human again. I walk out of the call center. I walk back down the narrow hallway of suite-sized doors. I make my way back out of the building and back to Eric's truck. I hop in.

"Well?" Eric says.

I try to keep a straight face for as long as I can and when I say for as long as I can, it was literally one and a half seconds before I break into a huge ass smile and laughter!

I can't hold it anymore, finally I shout out "I got the job! I got the job!"

Still smiling as if I just lost my virginity to Miss America, I tell him how much it pays and when I start. He gives me a high five. I'm *so* happy, and then my next thought creeps in.

How are you going to get back and forth starting Tuesday without money and without transportation? You probably have $10 in rolled nickels (if you're lucky) and it's only Thursday and you still have to eat two more times?

Geez, I can't seem to be happy for no more than sixty seconds these days. I choose to push that out of my head for now. Finding a job and better yet, an income can officially be scratched off my 'To Do List.' I have income. I have possibilities. I have hope. Incredible, by changing my mindset, I could give myself an additional sixty seconds of being happy. Hmm.

What to do next? Let's find a place to live. Why not? I'm feeling daring. Now that I have (not yet but starting Tuesday) an income to rely on I can start my search. It's time to find a place! It's time to turn this life around.

It's time to become a real person again! Goodbye homelessness.

It wasn't nice knowing you.

CHAPTER SIX
The jig is up

CHAPTER SIX
The jig is up

I MUST ADMIT, I can't believe how happy I am right now. It feels phenomenal to be able to say, "I have a job." After months of being homeless with a mix of being on the streets, eating out of garbage cans and sleeping in a retired office suite on the floor, I can say that I've finally found some hope. I'm positive for the first time in a long time. Truly, genuinely, positive.

After all my tirelessly hours of searching, posting, and sending out resumes only to have no one reply, weeding through the Craigslist scams after scams after scams, and bad interview after bad interview I have finally found a reputable company to work for! I'm finally going to be able to earn a check that I can count on to get me out of being homeless. This isn't the beginning by far, but it is a start.

Okay, next step. How am I going to get back and forth to work, starting Tuesday? I am very low on sidewalk change. Not a single dollar bill to my name and I do not have any transportation whatsoever. I know that Eric would help, but he's done so much for me already that I cannot bear to ask him for this. Some things you just should do on your own. I am determined to do this without him and show him that I can stand on my own two feet again. Not to be mean but to make him proud, to show him that all his effort and energy that he has put into me has and will pay off. Maybe I want to prove it to not only him, but to myself that I can do this. Either or, I will make him proud.

After checking, I only have ten bucks left of rolled up nickels and it's only Thursday. Oh boy, this is going to be tough because if I barely eat, eating just one thing a day, I don't know how I'm going to get through the weekend and make it to Tuesday on just ten bucks of rolled up nickels. I must find some way to get money for the bus to get back and forth from work until my first paycheck comes in. Yes, I said paycheck … so exciting!

After Interview Number Four we head back to his old office, a.k.a my crashing space, and once again I'm on Craigslist. I feel like celebrating—with what I have no idea —but there's no time for that, I should look for a place. Are there more important things I should be worried about, like looking for transportation routes? Maybe, but I have an income now and I should goal set. Find a place where I would like to live, even if I reverse engineer it, meaning find where I want to be five steps from here and work my way back, and do everything in my power to stay on track and get there!

I've put my high standards in place for the home I want to move into. That's the danger of hope, that even a hopeless man can have dreams and standards. There is no question of whether this is going to be a roommate situation, it *is* going to be a roommate situation. A situation where I am going to be moving into someone else's house and possibly renting a room from them in it. This is a far cry from a man that lived in a five-bedroom house in a very nice area of Las Vegas and drove luxury cars on the weekend. I look down at my feet. Yeah, I get it, but this is where I am at now and I should work with what I have been given. Not with what I once had. That's the past and this is now. I look back up. My thinking moves forward to today.

With my new job starting on Tuesday, making minimum wage and only having $10 in rolled up nickels, this will be tough. Tough because, even in a normal scenario, if I were to get a place on my own without a roommate, I would need to have $2,000 dollars to move into a two- or one-bedroom condo, leave a deposit, and turn on the utilities, etc. That is, as we both know, is a dream right now. I'm short $1,990 of that dream. Where I'm at right now is the kind of position where someone like me needs to find a room for rent. This would be ideal since I could move into an already existing two-bedroom condo with someone else for just a quarter of what's needed if I were to get a place on my own. If only I had a quarter of that. Remind you, the lease in Eric's charity homeless man's small ass office is up in two weeks. Talk about pressure which, by the way, is just now starting to find its way back into my life after all this time.

By this time, I am well versed in the Craigslist game and site. I know Craigslist like the back of my hand, like I've earned a doctorate in smelling out scams and searching and finding hidden gems on Craigs' inside hidden posts. Yep, those do exist. With my well-rounded experience with Craigslist, here is what I have found.

Craigslist is like working knee deep in the most grotesque pool of shit, without gloves on, blindfolded, with no sense of direction, being told about and told to search for, a .03 sized diamond solitaire somewhere along the bottom of it. You must search with your hands and without taking off your blindfold. Finding a place that I like that I can move into without any money is going to be a trip. I dig through Craigslist crap for hours and come up with a few good options. What I am looking for is a room for rent with its own bathroom, walk-in closet, granite counter tops, stainless steel appliances, a gym in the community, and in the nice parts of town.

Now, I know what you're thinking. "Really, Holis? You're freaking homeless. You're sleeping on the floor in an abandoned office without windows, without blankets, that was abandoned by your ex-boss. If you find *any* place on Craigslist, *any place*, you take it!" Sorry guys. I need a place where I can have my son over and be proud of where I live. I must shoot high, because if I shoot high and fall short of what I really want, I can't be that upset with myself because what I would have from falling short will still be pretty dope!

Plus, I now have dreams, possibility, and options now that I have income and a job! So, this imaginary place in my head with granite counter tops, — yes, out of my league right now, I know— is just what I want and I'm going to get exactly what I'm looking for. No words. End of discussion. So, leave me and my dreams alone for now, we're too busy dream-selling myself and discussing possibilities. With that being said I start looking.

I come across some nice rooms for rent but they all read "female only." Well, Craigslist is never short of old man perverts trying to entice younger women to come live with them with cheap rent and nice living environments. Check those air vents for micro cameras before you start changing and taking showers at night, ladies!

Oh, I forgot, even if I find a place, how am I going to get there? Just like my job interviews, I'm sure that it will take me a good four 'views' before I find something I like. Not only do I have to be mindful of my transportation issue, but I should be aware that I'm not going to be able to go see every single one. Any rooms from this point on I should be sure of before I go see them. How am I getting there? We'll have to figure that out later.

I find a few, so I start calling immediately. Ultimately, I start crossing off the list the potentials, the bad areas, one's without a gym (which if you saw how frail I am me right now, you would understand), and the ones that sound like my new potential roommate has kittens tied up in their bedroom. After crossing off nine out of the ten on the list and speaking to the owner, I find one. My new potential roommate seems decent. I call Eric and ask if he could take me. Wouldn't you know it? He's available and would not mind taking me! I am fucking love this guy! Then, there's a knock at the door.

I ask Eric over the phone, "Are you expecting company?"

Eric says, "No. Everyone knows that I gave up that office months ago."

I whisper, "I'll call you back." I hang up.

Too late, the voice on the other side of the door overheard me whispering. There's a man's voice demanding that I open the door.

Bang, bang, bang, bang, bang! Knocks on the door.

The voice on the other side of the door: "I know you're in there, open this door! Open this door now!"

What do I do? Seconds feel like minutes. I give up, he knows I'm in here, so I hesitantly crack the door open. It's the landlord.

He looks infuriated.

This is no ordinary landlord. He reminds me of the type of person who used to get beat up a lot in High School, and I mean a *lot.* A balding, frail, older man in his late forties who walks around the property with a Napoleon complex larger than this building.

He walks around the premises with a loaded pistol on his hip and he acts like a wannabe ex-Marine. His Jeep (of course he drives a Jeep) is covered with ex-Marine stickers and I've overheard him in passing once say that "He was never a Marine but supports them loyally." Now technically, I'm bigger than this guy (even in my frail condition as he stands in front of me) but, he walks around the complex with a gun on his waist and a chip on his shoulder, so I dare not mess with him.

Through the crack in the door I immediately ask," Can I help you?"

He has this look on his face like I just ran over his dog. He's pissed and is obviously not happy. The Property Manager snarls, "Who are you? What is your name?"

"My name is Holis. Can I help you?"

The Property Manager growls, "Are you living here?"

I give him the first and obvious answer. "Living here? What? No? Why?"

"Do you know the owner of the company who's renting this office from me?" the property manager asks.

I say, "Of course I do. You haven't answered me. What do you need?"

The Property Manager: "If you do know him, then what's his name?" And before I could answer, BOOM! He suddenly kicks the door open and barged his way inside the office. It's already tiny, but now it's feeling claustrophobic and I became pissed because he just invaded my privacy and has now just barged his way into my home without being invited. I become furious.

I protest, "You can't come in here like this! We pay rent here, we have rights!"

He makes his way over to the makeshift banquet table that was converted into a desk as if he didn't even hear me. He places five sheets of what looks like legal documents on the table and he says, "What the fuck is that smell in here? It smells like someone threw up on roadkill in here. You know what, it doesn't matter. This is an eviction notice. You need to sign this, and you need to get out of my office and off my property now! The neighboring offices that share walls with you, the people who pay rent to work here, who walk down this hallway and pass this office everyday are complaining about a foul smell coming from this room." I know exactly what and who he is talking about and I am seriously offended at this point. "What smell?"

The Property Manager growls, "The same foul smell I can smell right now. It's worse once you get into the room. It smells like someone has been living in this office."

I try, "I just told you…"

The Property Manager cuts me off.

"These office suites are for business purposes only. They are not for inhibiting and or sleeping in! Our bathrooms are not for personal bathing and you, sir, have been living here. You stink. You're disgusting and for that reason alone you must sign this document, vacate the office, leave my property and leave my building now! Take whatever shit that you have," he points over at my bag of clothing that is sitting in the corner, "and leave *now!*"

What could I say? I couldn't hide it anymore. I know what I look like. I know what I smell like. It's obvious that I wasn't working 'late nights' there. I obviously don't look like I've showered anytime recently. I was wearing ripped and torn clothing because I was trying to preserve my hand-me-down clothing for when I started looking at rooms for rent. And, well, what can I say? He was right.

It literally feels like as soon as I get three steps ahead, someone slaps me five steps backwards.

I look at his documents. Nothing major. Nothing that has the county logo on it or a law firm's name and address on it. Just simple eviction notices that you can download from Google. I briefly read them. I'm more embarrassed that I got caught, that the jig was up. I sign them all. There's nothing in the eviction notices that mentions he could sue me. What is he going to sue me for anyway? I have absolutely nothing.

After I sign them, I slowly pick up the papers and motion them as if I am about to hand them to him. Before I hand him the papers though, I use this moment to tell him the truth. I tell him that I have been homeless for four months now. That I have been living in this office for about three of those four months and that I have nothing left of my previous life. I wasn't looking for pity or charity, but I felt that he should know who he was kicking out. The room goes silent.

He finally says, "You have two days to vacate, and *trust me*, that's me being fucking generous."

He grabs the papers from my hands, turns his back and continues out of the tiny office, out the door he just kicked in and down the hall. He grabs the door handle to the door that exits the building, looks back at me, makes eye contact with me and screams with two fingers in the air, "Two days, *Motherfucker!*"Then he exits out of the building and I watch as the door slams behind him.

My happiness of finding a new job and being able to have an income for the first time in four months, and finally being able to see the light at the end of this tunnel called homelessness, has just been severely crushed. I was just casually looking for a place to live in for goal-setting purposes, but now that casual search has just turned into a dramatic four alarm fire. Me and my $10 of rolled nickels must make a move, literally. I need to search Craigslist right away and relentlessly to find somewhere to live before this asshole comes back to throw me out. I have two days, but knowing this asshole, less than two days to do it. The countdown starts, right now.

Who the fuck is going to let me rent a room from them and move in with just ten bucks of rolled up nickels as a deposit? I sigh heavily as I begin my search again.

What can I say? One step forward three steps back. This is my life trying my patience.

CHAPTER SEVEN
Ten dollars in rolled up nickels

CHAPTER SEVEN
Ten dollars in rolled up nickels

AS SOON AS THE LANDLORD LEAVES and the building exit doors slams behind him I pick up my phone and I call Eric.

"Bro, the building landlord just evicted me from your old office."

Eric sounds shocked. "What? Why? Really?"

"Yes!"

Eric asks, "What did he say to you?"

I stammered, "He told me that I smelled foul and that I smelled up the entire building! That I was basically squatting here and that living in the office suites here is basically illegal."

Eric says, "Wow!"

I exclaim, "I have to find a place to move! I have two places in mind that I found on Craigslist and if I find more tonight we should go see them tomorrow, please! Would you be able to take me to see them?"

Eric says, "Not a problem."

I sigh. "I can't believe I'm getting evicted again. Twice in four months. How does that happen?"

We both go quiet.

I finally say, "Thanks, I really appreciate it. I can't believe that he said that I smelled up the entire office building. I've never had anyone talk to me like that, ever!"

Eric says, "Sorry to hear that."

With no time to talk, we both hang up and I quickly jump back on Craigslist to look for more rooms available for rent and, of course, a miracle. Why a miracle? For starters, not only do I have to find a room for rent ASAP and get out of this office before they kick me out, but I remind you, I only have ten dollars in rolled up nickels to do it with. That's if I don't eat.

That is impossible, I must eat. After I grab a sandwich, I'm left with only five bucks in rolled up nickels to move with. This makes sense in my situation because if I buy a five-dollar foot long and I eat it carefully and slowly, I can split it into three meals over the next three days. Remind you, I start my new job on Tuesday and I was planning on treating myself to at least one bus ride back if I have a long day or if my feet hurt from walking that morning. Say goodnight to that dream.

Also, even if I do find a room for rent, who in their right mind is going to allow some stranger who called them off of Craigslist to come over and view the room available for rent? To move into the room with just $5 in rolled up nickels without a deposit? Yes, a miracle, and I'm in need of one right about now.

Right now, it's back to Craigslist once again and this time I'm searching for rooms for rent. I know, it doesn't make any sense. Why would I be searching for a room for rent without any money in my pocket? I don't know. What I do know is that for some reason the voice in my head will not allow me to do anything else. I can't explain how I know this but for some reason, I think that I'm going to find a place. As weird as it sounds, I think that I just might find a place and maybe that's where it all begins. Believing wholeheartedly, almost in an ignorant way, that it can happen. I guess we will see.

I find one looks good. It's $400 a month. East side and it's in the Ghetto. Who gives a shit? I certainly don't. I call, rented. Damn. I find another one, $350 a month in an even bigger part of the ghetto. I call, rented. Geez, who is renting these rooms?

I thought these would be slam dunks because of where they are located. I find another one, $550 a month. You can get your own condo in Vegas for $550 a month and this guy wants $550 for a room? This search is becoming pointless. With nothing to lose, screw it, I'm going to call. I look at the post again and he just piqued my interest. I take a further look at his post and damn it's nice. Three bedrooms, two baths, granite countertops, community gym, gated community, and on the very nice side of town. Just as I start to daydream about what it would be like to live there I'm suddenly slapped by reality. "You can't live there," said the voice in my head as it starts to scream at me. "You're a loser. Only winners live in that kind of neighborhood."

On top of having to be out in here in just a matter of days, after being recognized for sleeping in this office and washing myself in the public bathroom and being evicted twice in less than four months for smelling up the building, I start to become pissed. I don't know what happened next but all I can describe is a fire fueled anger starts to pass over me. I start to feel my heart rate rise from my feet and pass over my knee caps, my waist, up my arms, up over my head. I become extremely pissed, at myself. Not because of my situation, but because that voice inside my head that just said, "You can't live here, stop reading this ad, you're homeless." That voice reminded me of my ex-girlfriend and the final two years we spent together where she made it a personal mission to call me a loser every morning and every night before we went to bed. All the sudden, I'm back in that bathroom staring down at my toothbrush swirling around in that white toilet bowl again. I breathe and calm myself down by telling that voice in my head, "You're wrong, I'm not a loser. I deserve to live here just like the next person does. I will have this place. I will make it mine." Without hesitation, I call the owner of the condo and he answers.

Male, young, white guy. I would have to say around the age of 22, although he sounds much younger than that. Single guy and he works at one of the local casinos as a card dealer. We chat for a bit and he's pleased with me, for some reason, and he's anxious to rent out the room so we schedule a time for me to come check out the room tomorrow! Excellent, considering I have two days to get out of this office before the pissed off building manager kicks me out. We hang up. I back away from the computer, away from Craigslist and force myself not to look for any other rooms for rent. The search has been tiring and tonight's run in with the landlord, mentally draining.

I tell myself, "If I'm going to get this room for rent in the best part of town, with a community gym, gated, with a pool, security and granite counter tops, I'm going to have it all because I deserve it! I am *all in.*" At this point I decide. No more searching, I'm done with searching Craigslist ads for rooms for rent. I start to mentally tell myself, "There's no need to continue searching, I've found my place, period." I leave the desk alone, back up and lay on the ground. I pick up a book that I found in one of the filing cabinets and read myself to sleep. It's a boring book.

It's morning. I wake up still terrified from last night's encounter with the building landlord. Surprisingly, I'm quite positive though because I know and believe wholeheartedly that I found my new place! Don't get me wrong, I am fully aware that it's going to take a miracle for the owner to allow me to move in without paying one cent towards a deposit, rent, or anything for that matter.

There's an abrupt knock on the door. Great. The fucking property manager came back to give me another ten cents of his bullshit again. Without hesitation and, might I add, some bite in my voice I ask, "Who is it?"

A voice answers back. "It's me."

Oh, it's Eric. I open the door.

I say, "Dude, so tell me…"

He frowns. "Tell you what?"

"Well, does it smell in here? Does it smell like someone hasn't showered in months is living in here?"

Eric stalls. "Umm, well..."

I interrupt him. "Dude, don't worry about hurting my feelings, seriously."

He admits, "You can tell there is definitely a different kind of smell coming out of here. So yeah, it does, sorry."

I cringe. "Damn."

Outside of that we talk for a little bit about how the building manager barged in last night, belittled me and made me sign a vacate the property letter and him giving me 2 days— to vacate and quit the property. A contract in which I had to sign. It's starting to become apparent that my smell is starting to get to Eric. He's starting to make these weird faces and he's starting to move around a lot, like he is trying to find a good place to breathe. I guess the manager of the property wasn't lying.

I ask, "Want to go to Subway?"

Eric eagerly says, "Yes!"

I grab my journal and we walk to Subway. I always prefer to walk because you never know when you're going to get lucky and find a few quarters on the ground, maybe even a dollar bill.

We get to Subway, I get my breakfast, lunch, and dinner for the next three days in the form of a footlong sandwich. At this point, I've perfected a technique of how to get full on just three bites alone and to save the rest for later, by chewing my food until it becomes paste in my mouth. Then I swallow. Chewing like this tricks your stomach into believing that you've eaten more than you have and in return, you become full. No need to eat more than three bites. Tricks of the trade my friends!

We order and find a seat. I eat each of my three bites until they become paste in my mouth and in what seemed like just moments, Eric finishes his sandwich all in one sitting! It must be nice, I remember those days. He looks down at his watch, "Oh, we gotta go! You've got that appointment to see that room for rent at one pm right?"

I said hesitantly, "Yeah," knowing that going to this appointment to see this room for rent is either going to be a blessing, or a pure disappointment. I don't know anyone on this planet who is willing to wait thirty days to get paid and willing to let a stranger move into their house without paying one dime upfront. We leave. We hop into his truck and head up to see the room.

We arrive and when we do, of course, we come to the front of the community and to security gates that rise as high as the heavens in pure iron. Astonished, I call the owner and ask him for the gate code to get in. He gives it to me and Eric enters the code into the security pad and just like magic, those heavenly gates open. This moment I will later figure out becomes iconic to me. We make our way through the community looking for his building.

"There it is," Eric says.

We find a parking spot and park and Eric opens his door to get out. I don't open mine, partly because this could potentially be a big moment for me. I could potentially with one word or phrase, "Yes, you can move in" and just like that, no longer be homeless, but the real reason I don't open my door is because I'm afraid. He says, "We're here," as if I didn't know. I reply, "Hold on man, I'm scared, and I want to send the man upstairs (GOD) a message before we head inside." Religious or not, Spiritual or not, this moment can change everything and definitely needs a prayer.

Eric shrugs. "Um, ok."

I begin to pray myself, secretly. "Please God, please let this be the place! My new place. I'm so sick and tired of sleeping on the ground. Sleeping in Eric's office and not having a place to call my own. Please let this be the last place

I ever look for, homeless, ever again. Thank you." I cross myself, kiss the sky and open the door. I close my door behind me and we make our way to the condo. We wrap around the side of the building and find a pair of stairs. We walk up and stand in front of the door. With Eric behind me I knock. This dude in his mid 20's, we'll call him "Ben", answers and he says, "You must be Holis?"

I quickly reply so that he doesn't get his hopes up and think that the clean-shaven guy behind me, Eric, isn't the one interested in moving in. I even point at myself so that there's no confusion. "Yeah, that's me." Now, keep in mind, I haven't heard anyone acknowledge my name nor say my name in months and what really blows my mind right now is that I can't believe he's not looking at me like the rest of the world does. Like a complete mess. He's looking at me—and treating me, might I add— as if I walked in wearing an Armani suit! He didn't even care that I hadn't shaved my face. He didn't care that I had on torn clothes, even though I was trying my hardest to not look like it. I immediately like this guy! And from what I can see standing outside looking in over his shoulder I'm starting to like his place. He gestures for us to come in.

We go into the living room, which is beautiful. Large beige sectional sofa, an oversized ottoman, a 62" flat screen smart TV on the wall, open floor plan, great carpets. He motions us to the dining room, which is very impressive as well. Brand new dining room set made of dark cherry wood, enough room for eight guests. (If only I knew eight people. This would be an awesome place for us to eat!) And then comes the kitchen, the granite countertops, the stainless-steel stove and oven, oh, how I have missed you! The refrigerator matches the stainless-steel look throughout and what else do I see? See-through glass cabinets! Oh, I almost melt.

He motions us out of the kitchen, pass the dining room, pass the living room and down the hallway. We walk down the hallway and he shows me the third bedroom which was converted into a personal gym. My jaw drops. I haven't worked out in months and it's one of my long-time passions. Can this get any better? He shows me his room, though I'm not sure why, the laundry room, the guest bathroom and then finally the room for rent.

It's basically a closet. There isn't a walk-in closet but, there is a step-in closet. There isn't a private bath in this room, but the guest bath isn't too far of a walk down the hall. The room itself isn't that large, probably about 16 by15, not much bigger than my current situation but there is a nice, dark cherry wooden fan on the ceiling, and who would have guessed it, a window. Décor and a window to call my own, that I haven't had in such a long time. With all the amenities, plus where this condo is located, a great part of Summerlin, I'm guessing this room could go for $550 a month.

Now, in Vegas that is a lot to rent a bedroom, because you could easily grab a one-bedroom condo for that same exact price on the other side of town, without having to have a roommate. To be renting a room for what you can get on the other side of town, by yourself, without a roommate, you can see how this must be an enormous and nice place to live! I can't help myself, but ever since I saw the kitchen I was already starting to imagine myself living here.

And then the voice of negativity starts to come back again. *You can't live here, you're…* I cut it off before it has a chance to take over my thoughts and affect my mood. I badly want to fight for this place. I immediately make my way out of the bedroom to the kitchen. *You will not win.* I tell that stupid voice inside my head. *You are not my ex and I am not that person, not anymore. I'm a winner and to show you how much of a winner I am, I'm going to win this place!*

I have no idea what comes over me but, in this exact moment, I begin to spill the beans. I'm up front with the owner. I tell him everything, except for the fact that I'm currently homeless.

I tell him that I've lost everything. That I've lost my girlfriend of seven years, I've lost my son, my car, my job, and how I lost my five-bedroom house before my condo. That I am just now starting to rebuild again. Unbelievably I also tell him that I don't have any money to move in with, but I do have a job and I start on Tuesday. It pays minimum wage but it's something. I feel like I'm crying borderline begging at this point.
I try to convince him I'm worth a chance. "I promise, if you let me move in, I will give you my first week's paycheck as soon as I get it, I won't keep a penny. Keep it and use it as the deposit to move in! You can have all of it, it's yours!" Suddenly, I'm back in that barbershop again, where I begged for

that pair of hair clippers to get the rats' nest on my face and my hair before my job interviews. Man, these moments are starting to become more and more frequent.

Oh, and there it is…the Look. That same look the barber gave me in the barber shop but instead of a big black guy, it's a slender white dude. His head is slightly tilted to the left, as if saying to himself, *is this guy kidding me? Did he seriously come all the way over here to my house, with no money, just for me to show you my room and to waste my fucking time? Are you serious right now?*

The room goes completely silent for what feels like an hour. I'm fighting to hold back my tongue and the tears, because at this point I want to cry. I know I've wasted his time, but he has no idea how bad I want this. No words are exchanged at all. I turn and motion to Eric as if to say, "Come on, let's go." I turn my shoulders towards the door and start to make my way out. Then I hear, "Wait."
I stop dead in my tracks and I turn back.

"How much will you be getting paid per hour?"

I answer quickly, "$8.75"

"Are you going to be working full time?" Ben asks.

"Yes!"

He considers this. "How much will you make in your first two weeks?"

I blurt, "Roughly $700 after taxes"
He eventually says, "If you agree to give me your first two paychecks for the first two weeks and agree *not* to move in any furniture, just clothes only, I'll let you move in. You can have it."

I'm stunned.

I'm thinking, *Wait? What? Did he just say what I thought he just said?*

I just want to make sure. "Can you repeat that again?"

He says again, just as evenly as the first time, "If you agree to give me your first two paychecks for the first two weeks and agree *not* to move in any furniture, I'll let you move in. You can have it."

I turn to Eric for confirmation. I don't ask, "Did he just say what I thought he said?" Eric gives me the nod of approval. Ben did say it. I turn to my new roommate.

I smile. "You've got a deal!!!"

This dude has no idea who he's talking to. This is a win because I don't have any furniture! Shit, I don't have anything! I gladly accept his terms and we shake hands.
Just like that, I'm no longer homeless.
Did you hear me? *I'm no longer homeless!*

I'm so excited and so many feeling are rushing over me right now. And I get to keep my $5 in rolled up nickels! I think back to that prayer in the truck right before we made our way up the stairs. I look up at the ceiling fan in the kitchen and take twenty seconds to silently pray again. This time I say, *you do exist. You're amazing and thank you!* And just like that, I am no longer homeless.

I don't voice my next thought "Now, where is your bathroom again? Because my stink ass needs a shower!"

CHAPTER EIGHT

The introduction of Miss Puerto Rico

CHAPTER EIGHT

The introduction of Miss Puerto Rico

IT'S THE NEXT DAY.

I wake up on the floor in Eric's old office. The only difference from this day and any other day prior to last night will be the last time I sleep in this office ever again. Last night was the last time I will ever be homeless again. Speaking of which, I also signed a month-to-month agreement with my new roommate last night with the contingency that I cannot move any furniture in until I pay him my first two weeks of pay. I'm able to move in but I'm not able to move any furniture in. Easy for me because homeless people don't have furniture.

I can't tell you how amazing this feels. I have a home, guys, I have a home!

Lets backtrack for a moment. I was evicted out of my condo, evicted out of this office for smelling foul, I had lost my girlfriend, my family, my son, my ride, my job and my income. I had been living on nickels and dimes that I found in the cracks of sidewalks to eat food that I didn't have to fish out of a dumpster. I have one duffel bag of clothing and one friend, Eric. I have finally found a job and because of that job, found a new room for rent. Officially taking me out of homelessness and hopelessness and I have done what most would call the impossible. I'm not out of the woods yet by any means but I have possibility. I have hope. My newfound income doesn't hurt either.

Now, I know that I have found a job, even though I haven't started yet, I'm still going to look for work that pays better than $8.75 an hour. Yes, I just landed a new job, yes, I just landed a new place and yes, technically I'm no longer homeless and I should be grateful. I should be satisfied, but I'm not. I want more. I want better. I need better. Not just for myself but for the sake of my son. I need to be that shining example of falling hard on your face and not only getting back up, but surpassing everything I had been to become everything, I ever wanted to be. This starts with demanding better. Not asking but demanding better. So, it's back to Craigslist I go, to continue to look for a better job. Crazy I know, but this new me is revitalized, refreshed, and determined.

I send out my resume to what seems like a thousand companies with new job openings on Craigslist. Nothing has come back yet and after an hour my attention drifts off. How am I going to get to and from work next week?

Well, time to start planning my route! My new job starts Tuesday and I don't have any time to waste.

I search the address to my new condo (yay!) and then map it to my new work address. By car it's twenty-eight minutes and sixteen miles all together. Next, I check the bus routes and of course, there aren't any buses that travel to that part of Summerlin at all. Great.

I'm assuming that my new potential neighbors would never have a city bus driving through their communities, smogging (if that is even a word) up the place, ruining where they rest at. The surrounding communities in that part of town are gated two-million-dollar homes. These homes are quite large, and how does a man go from homeless to living next to millionaires get this lucky?

As it is, there aren't any bus routes near where I'm going to be living and I know this is nowhere near as big a problem as being out on the streets, but it doesn't take away from the fact that this is still going to be tough. This trying to get back and forth without a dime for transportation is going to be a hell of a challenge. Without money for a ride, that would mean that I will be potentially walking sixteen miles a day, or thirty-two miles round trip, to work and even if I left today, I still wouldn't be able to make it there on time on Tuesday…or will I? Then it hits me. How long does it take to walk a mile? I honestly don't know. I know I've walked a lot since losing my car, but I've never timed myself. Then I get an idea. I look down at my remaining five dollars in rolled up nickels. I look at my duffel bag in the corner, then back to my nickels. I got it! Dollar Store, baby!

I'll walk to the Dollar Store. Here's why this is genius. I'll walk to the Dollar Store which is just over 1 mile, I think, from Eric's old office suite and time myself. Not only that, but with five dollars in rolled up nickels, (which I know they will accept, I can get 5 boxes of Cheese crackers or some type of snacks or food for the next five days or so. This is perfect.

I know what you're thinking. "Why didn't you just walk to the Dollar Store for food instead of spending it at Subway in the first place?" You can't live off snack food, even though I'm forced to right now, plus I need the nutrients that you can find in a Subway sandwich to live off. Also, Subway is just fifteen feet away versus over a mile one way for the Dollar Store. Convenience wins. Anyhow, I search the address to the Dollar Store from Eric's old office. Just over 1 mile, yes! Perfect. I empty out my duffel bag of all my old, smelly clothing. I grab my saved-up nickels and take the first step out of the office to embark on my one-mile journey, with timing myself as a major priority.

Keep this in mind, I start off by walking down North Rainbow Blvd. This is sort of a major street in the local suburbs of Las Vegas. It is and can be very congested as times. People use this road to scoot from the Northwest part of town to the Southwest in no time and as I walk, I can't help but to think of how many people I know that are passing me by right now and if they even notice me at all. Since I haven't been able to shower or shave in months, I've grown out my beard completely and it looks horrendous. I can imagine them passing me by as I'm walking, noticing me and asking themselves "Was that Holis? No! Can't be!" This is a little embarrassing for sure. But who cares?

It's not as embarrassing as being homeless or convincing a convenience store clerk to take my one dollar of rolled up pennies at the register, so I can eat tonight. So, I brush it off and finally make it to the Dollar Store.

Time check. I look down at my phone, over a mile and a half in just under 20 minutes! And I walked my ass off! Naturally, I'm sweating. Showing up to work sweating will not work if I must walk there every day? Not good. I'll try not to walk so briskly next time. I sit down on a bench next to the Dollar Store to do the math. I think to myself, *lets see, if one-mile walking equals twenty minutes, then sixteen miles walking at twenty minutes per mile will take me five and a half hours.*" If I had to be at work at nine in the morning, I would have to leave my new pad and start walking at 4:30 a.m. at the latest. If I get off at five p.m. and it takes the same amount of time to walk home, that means that I will not be getting home until 10:30 at night. Combined to and from work, I would be walking thirty-two miles a day both ways. I'd be walking for over ten hours each day, Monday through Friday. I would be walking to work longer than it would take me to work my day. This is not a good solution for my transportation worries. Enough calculating for now, time to get something to eat.

I head inside the Dollar Store, excited to get my shopping started! Why? Because tonight I get to place all my purchased items in cabinets and a refrigerator! I haven't used cabinets or a refrigerator in months! I was kind of starting to miss these

things. I get a box of impostor Cheez-its, spaghetti, spaghetti sauce, rice and a gallon of water and with that it's officially goodbye to my last five bucks in rolled nickels. Goodbye to the last amount of currency I have to my name. I pack up my duffel bag with my Dollar Store food and make the long journey back to Eric's old office.

I make it back to the office suite. I look down at my phone. 22 minutes back. Not bad. Still about the 20 minutes it takes to walk a mile. I throw my bag down. I sit on the ground and revisit the idea of getting back and forth next week to my new job. Walking is out of the question and I've already asked Eric for way too much.

Then it hits me. Wait a minute, what about ride share? I've gone from homeless to getting a job, to getting a place to stay, I can work this out! I can do this.

What is rideshare? If you're not familiar with rideshare, it's an idea of two people coming together for one ride. The driver (the owner of the car) might be heading in one direction alone and could use some company. What they do is pick you up, if you are going in the same general direction as they are, and give you a ride in that direction if it's where they are going or if not close to. In exchange, they will accept donations in the form of gas money, tolls, food, some will even take trades, like laptops, depending on the distance. Some will rideshare from Los Angeles to New York or wherever.

There are ride shares here locally in Las Vegas that just ride around Vegas all day long looking for people to help split the cost of gas for a ride. Dangerous, yeah, I know. I'm broke too, yeah, I know. I have thirty-two miles a day to cover to and from work, plus I don't really have too many options. Time to hit up Craigslist once again! Why not? It's been good to me so far. I've found my first job since becoming homeless on Craigslist! I've found my new place on Craigslist. So why change a thing?

I get up and head over to the desktop again. I open Craigslist. I head over to the rideshare section and start to look up ads for local people offering rides. This is where it gets tricky. Not only do I have to find someone who is offering local rides, but also should find someone who will be willing give me a ride every day, Monday through Friday, without paying them one penny. I must convince them that they will have to wait three weeks before I can afford to pay them for driving me around.

Here's the plan: my paycheck for the first two weeks is already gone. It's my new roommate's, I owe it to him for letting me move in without paying rent or a deposit. The third week's check, that paycheck is open to be spent however, I please. This paycheck, from what I am planning, will have to go to my rideshare to get me to and from work. Not the whole check but I'm thinking about $300, which equates to $20 a day in gas money, from Monday thru Friday, every day, for the next three weeks. Now if you're doing the math, $8.75 an hour, is basically $8.00 an hour after taxes.

Take $8.00 an hour x's forty hours a week is just $320. $300 of which is going to whoever decides to take me up on my offer, leaving me with just twenty bucks after working there for three weeks. Twenty bucks.

Not a lot of money, but it's a lot more than what I have right now in my pocket and after everything that I've been through, I can live on just $20. Let's be honest, $20 in my pocket would be a blessing. I believe it's a fair deal.

I find twenty-five ads on Craigslist for ride shares and I start to call them up immediately.

Here is what I heard on the first fifteen calls:

"Fuck off"
"Are you crazy?"
"Would you do that?" Hang up.

I kind of expected that, but the next five calls after those were a lot nicer, but more along the lines of, "Call me back when you get some money in your pocket and I'll be more than happy to give you a ride anywhere then." The remaining five calls I decide not to take any more chances trying to explain my way around not having any money.

So, I told them the truth. I told them that I was homeless and that I am just now getting back on my feet and pleaded with them for them to give me rides to and from work, out of the good graces of their hearts. I begged, basically. Three said

"No thanks,'" but two were slightly interested! We decided to meet.

We would meet at the 7-Eleven, where I spent most all my rolled-up change on bags of Doritos to get by, because it was a well-known place and a mere ten feet from the office building I was sleeping in. It was the perfect place to meet.

Rideshare Driver #1, we'll call him Brady, was a younger black guy. He was a UNLV student looking to make some extra money for beer and books. He was down to give me rides but wanted collateral up front first. To be honest,

I became frustrated because it felt like I had just wasted my time, and because it was like he didn't believe me. That he didn't believe that I was homeless. I wanted to scream at him, "Are you kidding me, we talked for 20 minutes! Did you not listen to anything I said? You know my deal. You know I have nothing and need someone to give me rides to my new job upfront and need someone to give me those rides in exchange for $300 bucks later!" But I didn't say anything like that. I understood where he was coming from. He would have to trust that this smelly old guy, a stranger who was obviously going through some hard times would be able and willing to pay him $300 bucks three weeks from now. So, we exchanged numbers again and he said something that I am starting to get familiar with: "As soon as you come up with something of value that I can hold onto until you pay me my $300, then I'll do it." No hard feelings. He was truly a good guy. I hope he's does well.

Rideshare Driver #2, we'll call Miss Puerto Rico. This one is a woman. She's young as well, probably in her mid-20's, I think. She's slightly older than Brady. She's also a single mother with four kids, though I may be wrong about her being in her mid-20's. She's Puerto Rican from Bed Stuy, New York. In this moment, I only wish my Spanish was a little better than it was right now. After all, I learned it from Puerto Ricans. We start to talk about being back on the East Coast and how it's so different out here. I tell her about my trips I had taken to Puerto Rico, my trips out to Old San Juan and out to Maya-west. We had so much in common and hit it off almost immediately. She was here alone raising her four kids, with no family here on the West Coast and she had moved here for a brand-new start, to get away from her abusive ex-husband. She was amazing. She was an inspiration. She was so strong to be raising four children by herself in a town where she knew no one and had no help. She kind of reminded me of my mom who raised us under almost the exact same circumstances.

She agreed to give me rides to and from work Monday through Friday starting Tuesday of next week. She agreed to the $300 cash due at the end of those three weeks! Unlike Brady, she was willing to give me rides without wanting anything for collateral up front! This is amazing. She did have me make one promise, that I would never try anything or jeopardize her safety in any way. I have no problem with this and agreed completely and immediately. We laughed for a little while. I was making snap jokes about her being Puerto Rican, having four kids, and growing up in Bed Stuy. She took her jabs too!

With me being from "Dirty Jersey", it was easy for her too. It was fun. It reminded me of being back home.

With pleasure we shook hands, gave a quick hug and she went on her way. I double checked with reminding her like 35 times to not forget about Tuesday. I mean, what I can say? I'm excited! I was so happy and at the same time nervous and hoping that she wouldn't change her mind in between now and Tuesday.

This is just amazing! I have no idea how all of this is coming together or how any of these amazing people are coming into my life right now. All I know is that I'm celebrating inside. After months of being homeless I have a room for rent, I'm going to be taking a shower, I'm going to be shaving again. I have a roof over my head, I have five dollars in food, I have a job and I have transportation to and from it. The winds of change are now starting to positively blow in my direction! I feel amazing! I'm feeling human and Miss Puerto Rico is the shit.

CHAPTER NINE

You thought I'd be used to this by now

CHAPTER NINE

You thought I'd be used to this by now

IT'S DARK and an hour after letting my new ride share, Miss Puerto Rico, take off. I'm in Eric's office, sitting on the floor, writing in my journal and waiting for him to arrive so we can make our way to the first place I will be able to call home since going homeless. I've got my consignment clothes all packed up in my duffel bag.

I've got butterflies in my stomach from the sheer excitement of being able to have a roof over my head that I can call my own, and to be able to take a shower tonight! Wow, a shower. I can't believe those words came out of my mouth!

Suddenly, there's a single knock on the door. I'm like a rock. I mean, I don't dare to move a muscle and as I stare without even blinking, my thoughts race.

What the hell was that? Who was that? Was that someone playing a cruel joke? It sounded like someone threw a small bar of shower soap at the suite door. Or worse, is it the landlord? I say a quick and silent prayer. *Oh, please do not be the landlord, please, please, please, do not be the building landlord.*

Eric should be here any minute and I would not be able to take being thrown out of yet another place *again* without a ride or anywhere to go. Plus, this would be the second time in months. This is all becoming too traumatic for me.

Another single knock hits the door. I know for sure by now it's not the landlord. He would be screaming, "Are you out yet? You better answer me or I'm coming in!" And it's not a prank unless someone has decided to throw *two* bars of soap at this office door today. I know I'm supposed to be out tonight and that sleeping in this office suite on the office floor is not permitted. Not to mention, to use the landlord's words himself, that "Me smelling up the place" wasn't permitted, but it was the only place I could go. If it was the landlord, again those knocks would have been followed by him shouting in his "I-Am-God" voice, "You better not still be in there! I'm going to throw your smelling ass out on the street if you're still in there!" I give in. I slowly approach the door, put my hand over the door knob, (I left it unlocked, stupid) turn it slowly, open it, and who do I see?

It's Eric.

"What the fuck?" I say, with a huge grin on my face, glad that it wasn't the landlord. "You couldn't say, 'Hey, it's me, Eric! I'm here! Let me in!'" We both laugh. He knew what he was doing. It was a practical joke. He mumbles something, I mumble back, "Asshole," and we begin to grab my things and make our way out the office front door. Jokingly I say, "What a dick."

He asks, "Do you have everything?"

I look back at him like, "Really?"

He grins at me and then looks back at the ground as if to say, "Oh yeah, dumb question."

I completely take advantage of the fact that he barely just gave me a heart attack at the door just a second ago. "What are you going to do with that computer? The landlord is coming to put a padlock on the door in the morning and everything here is either going to be sold or thrown away."

He says, "Why do you ask?"

"Because, if that is the case and you don't need any of it, I would really love to keep the computer. It's the one that I have been using to find work and a place to stay on."

He pauses and eventually nods. "Yeah sure, it's yours, let's break it down and pack it up!"

I pause a moment, and then answer, "Awesome!" And I think a *"Yes!"* was in there somewhere as well too, internally of course.

We pack up the old desktop computer and carry it out to his car. I grab my duffel bag and throw that in his car as well, and

I make my way back to the office suite for one last look. I had to take one more look. I've slept on the floor in here, I've found my job here, I've counted countless pennies here, I've had many nights where I've gone to sleep hungry here. I've found my place here and I've called this place "home" for nearly five months.

As weird as it may seem, I'm going to miss this place. I take one last look around, turn off the overhead light and close the door behind me.

I wouldn't know, until we get in the car and leave, about how symbolic that was. I was closing the door behind me to a time in my life that I will hopefully never see again. I exit the building, hop in Eric's car and we head west of here to my new place. I'm hoping it is one of many trips. He starts the car and we begin to back out. We get to the end of the parking lot, we exit, and I can't help but to turn my head to look out the back window. I peek at the 7-Eleven. The place where I stood (ironically) next to the garbage can ignored by mass population of people. I used to just stand there and be and imagine the lives of those who used to come in for a quick coffee and a sandwich. I used to imagine how amazing their lives must how lucky they were to have friends and family. I reminisced about Subway sandwich shop. I looked back at the building. Then I turn, sit in my seat and look forward out the front windshield. Looking towards the future.

From this point on, that's all I'm going to be doing. Looking forward.

We take our trip onto the highway and up West Summerlin Parkway. It's easy to get to my new place now. With just one showing, I was so excited that I've pretty much memorized it. We get to my new place and the iron gates reaching as high as the heavens, built to keep people like me, the once homeless, out of here, are the only thing keeping me away from a place I can finally call my home. I enter the gate code—excuse me, MY new gate code—and the gates begin to open. As they do, I think, "Finally!" and "I deserve this." This is the beginning to a new and great life for me, I just know it. A smile reaches my face as we enter my new community.

We take a few rights, and then lefts, and finally reach my new building. We park. I grab my stuff. Eric grabs some computer components and we head towards my new place. We head up the outside stairs, I ring the doorbell and my new roommate answers. I think to myself, *please do not answer and say, Gotcha! I was only kidding!" or anything like, "Sorry, but I've changed my mind about you living here."* Please don't, anything but that. But he doesn't. Instead I hear, my new roommate say casually, with a smile on his face, "Hey! What's up!" I immediately think, *Phew, that was close. Well, thank God, a smile is always a good sign!* He didn't change his mind about me being able to move in without paying one penny towards rent or security! As soon as I step over the threshold of the front door and into the living room I knew I was in. I knew that I had reached home plate. *Try changing your mind and kicking me out now buddy! It's going to take the National Guard and fifteen grenades to get me out of here!*
I hit my room to throw my bag down and head back out with Eric to get the rest of the computer components. Come back. Drop them off in my new room. Eric, being the introvert that he is, is not used to opening up to strangers, so he quickly makes his way to the front door, says goodbye and I close the door behind him. Wow! I just closed the door to my new apartment right behind Eric for the very first time in months. I had to let out a sigh.

While I'm standing there with my hand still on the door knob my new roommate starts to look confused, as he sits on the living couch. He finally gets the nerve up and asks, "Is that it?" I think to myself, *if only he knew.*

He continues," No boxes? No clothing, no dressers or blankets? No desk or a bed? Is that seriously all you have?"

I take the liberty to remind him, "Well, you did say that I couldn't move anything big in until I've paid you my first two paychecks first."

He remembers and says, "Ah yeah, that's right. Okay, cool."

I don't know yet, but this will not be the first time I hear this question. Not just from him, but from others who will soon come to visit me.

I then respond with, "I'm going to take a shower, it's been a long day." He looks even more confused as if to say, "Why are you telling me that you're about to take a shower?" "It's your own personal bathroom." I'm so ecstatic about being able to take a shower that I felt like I had to tell somebody!

I head back to my new room. The first thing I do is grab my duffel bag and head to the laundry room. It's the first time that these clothes have been washed in five months. No soap. Who cares?

I dump them into the washing machine and place the washer on wash and head to the bathroom. I'm quickly reminded again because it had been so long, that throwing clothing in the wash right before you're about to take a shower can be considered the ultimate no-no. I take my clothes off, hit the shower and get about thirty seconds of hot water before everything goes cold, frigid! I scream out, "Gawt dangit!" and laugh silently with myself. *Come on Man. Laundry, shower, never at the same time. You know this!* Just like my laundry, my shower is cold water and no soap but who cares. I love it! I'm standing in a shower and showering. I'm washing my entire body! I let out another scream, "Woo hoo!" If my new roommate could hear me, he's probably second guessing the decision he made to allow me to move in right about now, but as far as the shower, I absolutely love it! It's a feeling of liberation that I haven't felt in such a long time.

I get out of the shower and realize I don't have a towel. I was so excited about taking a shower that I forgot to figure out how I was going to dry myself off. I spot a guest towel hanging on the towel rack. I grab the it off the towel rack and wrap myself in it to dry off. For some reason, I cannot help but look in the tub. I don't know why, but something was telling me to turn around and look. So, I did. Of course, it's filthy, and there's a spectacular ring around the tub like I've never seen before. Yes, a ring around the tub and I took *a shower!* Not a bath, a shower! It looks as if someone had washed years off their body in tub.

Without hesitation, I run to my room, come back with my phone and take a picture. After taking the picture, I stand back in acknowledgment. *I can't believe that I was carrying around that much dirt on me,* I say to myself.

It looks like what the tub would look like if three kids who were playing in the mud all day long just took a bath together and got out. That's how much dirt is in my bathtub right now. *This is embarrassing. Not to mention, how am I going to clean this up?*

I find some cleaning solutions under the sink. Thank God for that and I begin to clean the tub. This easily could have been another "fuck you" moment, like the moment I had in the office building with my toothbrush and the toilet. And I could have easily said "Fuck your dirt, I'm clean now!" but I'm so happy I choose not to go into all of that right now. So, I head back to my room. I lay down on the ground, on the carpet. Feeling so clean, so elated, so content, I close my eyes and, naturally, drift off to sleep.

The weekend passes like minutes. I'm getting along with my new roommate well and I have clean clothes. I've eaten two of the four boxes of Mac'n'cheese, one a day, that I've made without butter or milk because I couldn't afford it at the time, and behold, it's Tuesday. It is day one of my first new job since getting back on my feet! It's seriously five in the morning and I have not been up this early in a long time. It's roughly 5:10 a.m. and my phone goes off. It's my Miss Puerto Rico. Ah, she remembered, and most importantly, she didn't back out or change her mind about our ride share agreement. I love this girl! I'm astonished that she has four kids. She's a single mom and still found time to pick me up at 5:10 in the morning. Me. A stranger, might I add, to take me to work on my first day. I start at six. No time to waste. I must get dressed.

It's 5:15 in the AM on the dot and she's here. I'm dressed in my best clothes that I can muster up to make a good first impression. I grab my key, (I'm so excited to be able to say that) and two cereal snack bars that I bought at the dollar store. This will be my breakfast and lunch for the day. I head out the front door. I turn around and lock the door behind me. I meet her downstairs, hop in her car, and we take off for my first day of work.

We try our best to chat a little bit being as tired as we both are. We try to continue where we last left off, about her being the stereotypical Puerto Rican single mom from New York City and having four kids. Us both being from the same tri-state area, her New York and me North Jersey, we both have the same sense of humor and same attitude. Hey, if you can't laugh at yourself, then who can you laugh at? We laugh a little. It helps wake us up and get the morning started right. She entered the address to my new job into the navigation app on her phone before we left my place, so our ride was pretty much carefree. We finally get there, we enter the parking lot and her car rolls to a stop. I look up at the office building in front of us, knowing what's inside, my first day of work since going homeless. I'm petrified, like I'm six and it's my first day of school. I almost wanted to yell out, "But Mommy, I don't want to go to school today!" But I'm not six and this isn't school. It's real life. Thoughts race through my head like it's the freak'n Indianapolis 500.

What happens if my new co-workers don't like me? What happens if I don't make the cut? What happens if... I cut myself off. I look at her as if to say, "What do I do?" She looks at me as to say with all her New York City attitude, *"Can you get the fuck out of my car so I can go home and take care of my four children please?"* I smile, then nod as if to say, "'You're right!" and say out loud, "Thank you for the ride, see you at four!" She smiles.

I get out of her car, close the door behind me and hear her start to take off. With every step, my heart pounds more and more. The anxiety begins to grow with every step. Just as I reached my sixth step, I have a moment of clarity. I look around and start to notice that the parking lot seems empty for a six am start time. That thought is quickly taken over by, *I'm almost at the front door,* and the "what if" questions start to return. I get to the building. I find their suite and reach for the door. I grab the handle on the left glass door. It's locked. It's not opening. I try the handle on the right glass door. That's locked too. What's going on here? I try both door handles at the same time.

They're *both* not opening. What the heck is going on here? I look back to see if my ride share was magically still here. Nope she's gone.

As I look back at both doors, door handles still in both hands, I just so happen to look to the bottom of the right-hand side door and see their *new* business operating hours. They don't open until 8:30 am.

Internally, I'm raging. *New business hours? You've got to be kidding me! Seriously! Pshhhh, great! So, you're telling me that I must wait out here with two cereal bars for two and a half hours until you open? How is this possible? My boss told me six a.m. Tuesday! I know he did!*

Well, I calm down and quickly come to two realizations. One, it's dark because the sun has yet to come up and two, I'm obviously not getting in any time before 8:30. Oh, and I'm starving, but I'm used to that by now. Who would have thought to call your new job the day before you start to make sure they didn't change their business hours? I mean, really.

Argh. My next realization is that it looks like I'm hanging out here for a while.

Welcome to your first day of work Holis.

CHAPTER TEN
No barriers

CHAPTER TEN
No barriers

IT'S BEEN A FEW HOURS.

At this point I have sat on the ground, brought my legs in close to my chest and wrapped them with my arms. Around this time of year, it gets cold here in Vegas in the mornings so I'm trying my best to stay warm. The sun has come up, but it's not enough to help. I don't have a jacket, just this thin shirt that resembles something short of a sweater is all I have to keep warm, but it's better than nothing. While I have been waiting for the building to open and start my first job since going homeless, a few more cars have filled the parking lot. People have gotten out of them and made their way to their respective workplaces. Not one of them worked in my building, though. I'm sure it must be closer to 8:30 am by now. I've been sitting here since six and I'm too cold to take my phone out of my pockets to check, but it should be closer to 8:30 am. It just has to be.

A new car to the parking lot rolls in, they find a parking spot next to my building and the driver gets out. Oh wait, what's this? It looks like he's coming my way. He is! *Finally!* I say to myself. I hope he works in one of the other office suites on my floor and not in my actual office. I imagine how embarrassing it could be to explain why I was sitting outside for two and a half hours in the cold, waiting for the building to open, and why didn't I just go home and come back. The talk around the water cooler later in the day I imagine: *Yeah, I came up the stairs and he was just sitting there shivering. He reminded me of somebody who might be homeless, except he was wearing nicer clothes.* Not too far from the truth there, sir.

He came up the stairs, my suite is on the second floor, and by now I recognize that he's not my boss. As he comes up the stairs, when he isn't looking, I do my best to stand up, grab my phone out of my pocket and pretend that I wasn't just sitting here for over two hours waiting for someone like him to come along and open the doors, so I could sit inside and wait for my office suite to open. He makes his way to me. *Yes!* He looks at me, I look at him, I nod, he nods and then he goes into his pocket. He pulls out a pair of keys and raises them to the door and unlocks it. Turn and click *I'm in!* I wait for him to make his way through the doors. I count to three and go right in, right behind him. I take two steps inside and I can feel the warmth from the heat almost immediately. I wait to see which suite he's in. He walks down the long hallway and stops in front of suite number 299. Good, he's not a fellow employee of mine. Our suite number is 308. My secret is safe, for now! That was a close one.

As soon as he makes his way inside and closes the door behind him, I hit the floor again. Knees tucked in and arms wrapped around my legs. I'm in the heat now, but I'm still freezing. More and more people start to make their way into my building and to their suites. It's got to be 8:45 by now. Where is everybody? I look at my phone, it's 8:29 am. Then something catches my eye and I look out the glass doors. Who do I see? My boss, the guy that hired me and he's on his way up the stairs now. *About time, son!* I think, my Jersey coming out strong. Obviously, he's psychic because as soon as he enters the building the first thing he says to me is "Been waiting long?"

Now, you can imagine what I really felt like saying here but I didn't. Just a quick, "No, not that long at all," came out. He says, "Yeah, we start at 8:30

on Tuesdays." He looks at me as if waiting for me to say something, and when I don't, he says, "Okay, well then, follow me." I follow him down the long hallway. We get to our suite, number 308. He goes into his pocket to pull out a pair of keys, and unlocks the doors to let us in.

We're the first ones in the office. *Does this mean I get to pick my desk?* I didn't ask it, but it does cross my mind. He picks up his hand and points. "That will be your desk." he says. It's the very first desk you see when you step into the office. My desk practically blocks the front entry door from opening all the way. If you were to open it up wide enough, you could probably take out my left elbow in one shot. I ask, "Are there any other desks? Preferably one where I get to keep my left elbow if a door opens up too quickly?" My new boss answers, "Not now."

Ironic really, how I find myself in yet another office suite, but at least this time I don't have to sleep on the floor. I sit down and get settled in. By this time people start to trickle in. It's a small office, there are only ten desks total, including my boss's. It's a very casual atmosphere here, no dress code and by nine a.m. all ten desks are eventually filled and the day begins. The boss doesn't mention one word, he doesn't introduce me as the new guy nor does he stare down at those who were late.

When I said casual atmosphere, I mean this is Casual. He eventually comes over and gives me a few passwords on a single sheet of paper and shows me how to log into the platform to take calls and listen in on others as they're on their calls. And he says, "There you go, let me know when you're ready to get on the phones." I'm blown away. I think, *Wait? What? That's it? That's the extent of your training?* I don't say anything. I bite my tongue and think, *I guess this is how they do things here.*

I'm a little upset about the so-called training so far. Why? If you are in a position of management, like a supervisor, I am a firm believer that your sole duty is to be deeply involved in developing people and that no matter what you are paying them, whether it's $8 an hour or $180 an hour, everyone deserves proper and proactive training. Back that up with a caring and determined supervisor and a training mentor, a veteran employee who knows the ropes and is accountable for your success as a new employee, then success is yours! I believe in this because people need to feel valued at any rate an hour. Not here, though. I guess you can't expect NASA style training on what $8 an hour pays.

Our boss takes off for lunch, which I think is another thing managers shouldn't do. You should spend your lunch eating a light snack while you walk the floor and see how your employees are doing, in my opinion. Other employees are now starting to come over and introduce themselves. I find out within seconds that they wanted to come over and gossip with the new person. The conversation very quickly comes up that our boss is not much of a boss at all. Meanwhile, I haven't even mentioned my name yet. They just come over and start to get knee deep in it with me.

This is worrisome, because it shows that there might be some animosity amongst the tribe members and I don't need negativity in my life right now. They tell me how he became the boss, that he was a sales rep turned sales superstar, turned manager and then finally turned site director by the *real* owner of the company, who I hear lives a very comfortable life in LA and is also our boss's best friend. Now it all makes sense…if it is the truth.

The boss comes back from lunch and the other employees take off like roaches when the lights come on, scurrying away from my desk. The boss comes in and takes his seat. The day is flying by fast! My lunch has passed, I ate my snack bar at my desk while monitoring others on their calls, the afternoon comes, and it's now close to four in the afternoon. My boss, whom we will now call Josh, comes over at 3:30pm and says," How was your first day?" I say, smiling, "Good!" He mentions "Well, it's your first day and I don't want you to get burnt out. Why don't you pack it up early? And I'll see you tomorrow at 8:30 a.m. sharp." I say, "Oh, you mean like, nine a.m. sharp? Like the four out of ten that walked in this morning late?" I'm met by silence. Apparently, he doesn't get New York City and Northern Jersey sense of humor. It's my first day, I should stop.

Now that I think about it, I guess my joke was slightly serious. It does upset me to see people squander opportunities. Yeah, you're making eight bucks an hour, but there are people here who are making eight an hour plus twenty-five percent commissions. Not me, obviously, being new, since my commission scale doesn't start until after I've been here ninety days, but if you're making commissions, that by itself should deserve respect. Just like people who buy nine-dollar sandwiches, eat three bites and throw the rest away. This, for obvious reasons, just pisses me off. Don't get me wrong. If it wasn't for people like that I would have never eaten, but wasted talent, wasted food, it just gets under my skin. We're all too smart to be so wasteful.

My next thought is, *I wonder if Miss Puerto Rico can pick me up early?*

I pack up my notes from the day, my journal, shutdown my computer and head out. I get outside the now famous glass doors to our building where I was waiting just seven hours ago in the cold for two and a half hours before the office opened, reach down to my phone and text Miss Puerto Rico.

She sends a text back, "Can't be there until 4pm" To her defense, I am getting out slightly earlier, so I wait for the second time today. I find a nice place outside far from the building and far from where my fellow employees would be parked or would see me waiting for my ride. I sit on the curb, open my journal and start to write about my day's experience.

Now, I know that I only made $56 today, eight dollars an hour times seven hours, and less than that if you subtract my lunch. Let's be honest, eight bucks an hour is (to most) complete crap money. I can't believe that it's still legal to pay someone this rate of pay in exchange for their time, but here's the thing: it's funny, even though I only made just eight bucks an hour for my time today, I feel productive right now! I feel like I just put together a rocket ship by hand for NASA, even without the training! That's how productive I feel. I've earned something today which I haven't been able to do in a long time. Yes, again, it was only eight an hour but you're missing the point here. Eight an hour today will soon turn into eighteen an hour later, which will then turn into eighty an hour much later and so on and so forth. Whether it's here or somewhere else, it's all about raising your productivity in yourself and starting somewhere, and starting somewhere is exactly what I am at.

A half hour passes quickly. Miss Puerto Rico arrives and she's on time too. She's so awesome. We kick it for a bit on the way home. We chat about whatever. Mostly about being back in New York and what we would be doing if we were still there. I spent all my summers in New York. I must admit, I love Vegas so this was more of an entertaining conversation than serious. At least for me it was. For her? I don't know. I think a part of her still wishes she was back in New York. I can attest, I miss the grittiness, the rawness, the realness, and attitude and the people of Northern New Jersey and New York, but it's the kindness of the people here which is why I was able to get out of my situation so quickly. Yeah, I miss New Jersey but I love Las Vegas.

We get to my place—can you believe it? I just said "my place! "— and she drops me off.

I remind her, like I do, fourteen times that I start tomorrow at 8:30 in the morning and to be here at eight a.m., *not* six a.m. She laughs, as if to say, "Yes, I got it the fourth time you said so." She waves, drops me off, and takes off. I head upstairs.
I open the door, drop my stuff on the countertop and head to the kitchen to begin filling a pot with water. I place the pot on the stove and grab a box of mac-n-cheese out of the cabinet. I'm absolutely starving at this point. Remember, all I had were two granola bars to eat all day. In the meantime, I head to my room with my training notes and my journal to change and finish writing today's entry.

After my food is done I'll get back on Craigslist. At this point I can't stand Craigslist. I have a love hate relationship with the website right now. I found my job and my place on it, but I can't stand being on it anymore. I search for better paying jobs, submit my resume a few hundred times, I also search the free section for a bed mattress and box spring and check the barter section, for people who might need moving labor in exchange for some form of transportation, a bike, a scooter, anything.

I start to feel this strange appreciation for what I went through, still going through, start to come over me. Now that the hard part is over, I am nowhere close to being finished, but I start to recognize that after going through what I've been through, I can do anything. There are truly no barriers. That this life is amazing and that with a plan, determination, and sheer force of will, I can truly have everything and anything I ever wanted.
Not that I didn't know this before, but this time around there is proof and an appreciation for the process when back then, all that mattered was getting to the end result. I'm taking a vow now that I'm going to appreciate everyone that comes into my life, every connection, every friend, every family member and every acquaintance. I'm going to let them know, no matter what, how

special they are, even if they don't recognize it in themselves yet. I'm going to live to inspire others to let them know that change is possible and if they just believe in themselves that they can and *they will do* remarkable things. This isn't me signing off, this is me signing on! Signing on to take that responsibility and place it on my shoulders. There's a brand new me in town and world, I hope you're ready for it, because here I come!

But first, I should find a better paying job on Craigslist. When it comes to saving the world, I'm going to need a lot more than just eight dollars an hour to do so.

So, world...*you'll have to wait*...for now.

CHAPTER ELEVEN

I'm just practicing

CHAPTER ELEVEN
I'm just practicing

THINGS ARE STARTING TO COME TOGETHER.

It's been a couple of weeks and work is good, but I still eat, read and practically live on the floor in my bedroom. I do not have a bed yet, just like when I was homeless, I'm still sleeping on the ground. Eight dollars an hour doesn't get you a whole lot these days. Between paying for ride shares and paying my roommate back for letting me move in without giving him any security or rent up front, I'm paying my dues and there isn't much room for anything else. My computer is also on the ground too because I do not have a desk to put it on, but on the brighter side of things, I've paid off my roommate! Also, I'm on my third week at work and I'm about to give my ride share her three hundred dollars for giving me rides to and from work over the past three weeks. Awesome! And I'm even making friends at work, which is a weird feeling because I haven't had anyone show any interest in me, as a friend or whatever, for a very long time.

You know what the hardest part is about being homeless? It's not the part where you don't know when you're going to eat again. It's not the part of not knowing what you're going to eat again. It's not, not having a place to go home to at the end of the day. It's not the fact that you're sleeping on the streets; it's not even the fact that at any time you could be attacked by someone with a mental illness who is also homeless. It's not the cold nights. It's not sleeping in public bathrooms. It's not eating out of garbage cans. The hardest part about being homeless is how other people treat you, while you are homeless. It's the ones that are walking down the street and see you coming their way and purposely cross the street so that they don't have to pass you in fear that you might try and rob them or, God forbid, ask for a dollar.

It's the ones that that come to the light at an intersection and see you standing there with your 'Anything helps' cardboard sign who immediately roll up their windows, pick up their cell phones, and pretend that they are on the phone so that they don't have to look in your direction or make eye contact with you. Those are the ones that really hurt. The worst ones are the ones who not only roll up their windows at the intersection, but also immediately lock their doors as soon as they see you. "Click" goes the automatic door locks, then: "Don't look in his direction. Don't look." I'm sure that's what they think. The hardest part of being homeless is not being homeless. It's how others who try their best to wish you away, to make sure you disappear, even when you're standing right in front of them that really hurts. We're not a bad dream, we're people.

Luckily for me my new roommate has a taste for fresh baked goods and is completely *fucking wasteful.* I can't tell you how much this gets under my skin. Let me give you a little insight to who my roommate is. He in his late 20's and, as some would say, has the personality and habits of a spoiled rich kid. I don't know if this is true or not, but it might explain his wastefulness. Like I mentioned before, he has a taste for baked items. Specifically, baked items from Fresh 'n Easy and Vons and Smiths. He buys fresh baked cookies from the bakery practically every day. Every day when I come home from work there is always a fresh box of something on the countertop. Here's an example of what I mean. Monday through Friday he would get a box of twelve freshly baked cookies, he would eat a few of them, then let them sit out on the counter for a good day and then proceed to throw them in the garbage. They would never be any more than three days old and in the garbage, they would go, and it's a good thing too! If only he knew how many times I've gone into that trash. If he knew how I've eaten and hid those cookies in my room just to eat them later, he would probably be appalled. They were so good, though. Little does he know, if it wasn't for those cookies I would have probably died of starvation, ten times over. I've eaten three-day old cupcakes that he's thrown out. I've eaten old bananas, boxes of stale crackers, you name it. I've eaten it out of his garbage a dozen of times and I cannot tell you how thankful I am for wasteful rich kid roommates.

Even to this day I'm sure he probably has no idea why I enjoyed taking the garbage out so much. He probably thinks he has the absolute *cleanest* roommate on the planet, the way I enjoy taking the garbage out every night. Obviously though, it was because I was hand-picking what he had thrown away to save and eat in my room later. Nine out of ten nights, this was the only way I would have something to eat. This was basically how I ate after my Dollar Store food ran out and during the entire month I was paying people back from my paychecks. Hey! Don't feel bad for me, digging for something to eat out of the garbage in my own kitchen is Disneyland compared to digging for food in the dumpster behind any restaurant! Plus, one man's trash is another man's treasure, and I was taking full advantage of it.

Some might say, "Wasn't there anyone that could have helped you with food? Why didn't you get to a mission or homeless shelter for food?"
I didn't know where to go for help. I've never been homeless before and I wasn't hanging around other homeless people, so these resources were unknown to me. I never knew where to go or who to ask for a sandwich when I was hungry. I've always made a sandwich in my kitchen if I was hungry and to be honest, I was too ashamed to go to missions, even if I knew where they were. During this time and, of course, even right now, there is a part of me that feels like not only did I fail everyone around me down, but I've also failed myself. Big time. By the time I had internet access to find out where these resources were, I already had a roof over my head, even if it was sleeping on the ground in Eric's abandoned office. If I went down to eat at the mission, I would have been taking a meal away from someone who really deserved it, someone who probably didn't have a roof and needed it more than I did. Thinking like that, I somehow feel like I've contributed to the greater good. Somewhere, right now, there is a hungry man with nowhere to go in a mission eating a hot meal because I'm not there. Eating the meal he otherwise would

not have had if I was there, and that makes me feel good! Starving or not, the idea alone fills me up.

I know what you're thinking, "How did it ever get this bad? "Well, because I was ashamed, depressed, lost everything, mentally exhausted, and thanks to my ex, I was totally convinced that I was a complete loser. I can't honestly tell you where it started. It was a snowflake that turned into eight feet of snow fast. Let's just say that I've made some bad decisions and took a left where I should have taken a right. I put friends and family last, I got desperate, I started making even dumber decisions based off desperation, and when things became really bad (selling furniture just to make rent), it steamrolled into making even worst decisions out of desperation, one after another until I eventually lost it all.

I could blame it on my ex-landlord for not having any compassion, I can blame it on the economy, I could blame it on my old boss for firing me at a time when I was already a month behind on my rent, sure, why not? But, I'm not going to do that. Blame would just put the responsibility on someone else when the responsibility is mine and mine alone. That would be irresponsible for me, plus it would not get me to where I want to go in life. I must take responsibility for the decisions I have made. If I ever want to get to where I am going I must take responsibility of where I am in life right now.

I'm not going to get to where I need to be by blaming my misfortune on the circumstances that happen around me! That's complete bullshit and I would be lying to myself if I did. That would be an excuse and we're not about excuses, not anymore. Hold on a second, I've got my hand inside our garbage and I'm touching something that feels quite familiar...Oh wait, is it? *Yes! It's cookies!*

I've been outside for an hour now and it's about time. I throw the rest of the garbage in the dumpster and hide the cookies under my shirt as I make my way upstairs. I'm hiding them because my roommate is in the living room watching TV and I don't want him to see that I've been digging in the garbage and eating his throw away food. I enter the front door, without saying one word to my roommate I make my way to my room, very, very quickly. I devoured four cookies almost immediately. I literally inhaled them. I can't even remember what they looked, smelled or tasted like. That's how fast they were gone. The only reminder I have that I ate anything at all, is the leftover chocolate chip crumbs on my fingertips. Even they taste good. I still have five left and the four that I just ate should get me through dinner with my co-workers tonight! So, I'm good.

I look at my phone. Dang it's almost seven p.m.! I should get these crumbs off my fingertips and take a shower, so I do. It still feels good to know that I can take a shower whenever I want. As I wash up, I can't help but think about my li'l man. I can't help but wonder how my son is doing. How my ex is doing (she is my son's mom after all). It's been since September since I've seen my son. I wonder if he will remember me. I really fucked this whole thing up. I just would like to know if my son is doing well and how she's doing since everything fell apart, after I failed her. After all, this was my fault and I haven't seen the both since the day of our eviction. I do know where she works, and I could always go down to her job but at this point, in her tiny office, I'm sure they all know what happen and I bet they wouldn't let me within two feet of her desk.

Before the eviction, while I was trying to figure things out and fix them, after it had become too late, she already knew and had the insight to start looking for other resources. Her mom had already come down from Idaho to watch my son during the day because we could no longer afford daycare. She would go to work and I would hit the strip to yet another business meeting to hustle and find a way out of this mess.

When she returned, she always had pages of Craigslist For Rent postings printed out. Even from a distance, I knew that they were ads that she had printed out for condos for rent. We never spoke of it, but a part of me wished that she was being proactive, helping, and bringing me with her. I knew this wasn't the case. She was too pissed at me at this point, too far gone. After all, the person that was supposed to be the breadwinner was no longer making bread. That same person put her and our family last and at risk of becoming homeless.

That by far was the *second* hardest sentence I have ever had to write in my entire life.

As I shower, I decide what to do. I'm not going to wait for the magic moment when I'm back on my feet. Next payday, after I've paid off my ride share and have a few hundred bucks in my pocket, I'm going to go down to her job (whether her colleagues like it or not) and hand her a few hundred bucks as a peace offering. I'll ask her about scheduling a time for me to see my son. Besides, I'm used to surviving on just twenty bucks a week, if not less, so what's another $300 out the door? Plus, it's not really hers, it's his and deep down, he's worth it and he's mine. Not to mention *it's the right thing to do.* Hope my roommate hits up Vons soon 'cause it looks like I'll be going through his garbage and eating his three day old cookies for a little while longer!

As far as tonight is concerned, though, tonight is going to be awesome! I've got plans tonight to hang with one of my co-workers. It is safe to say that I'm excited! Even if I have nothing in my pocket (I'll just take a water please), it's more important to me to be out somewhere socializing with a new friend than to worry about what they will think about me when I can't order a beer or anything to eat. Plus, I have the excuse of, "I just started working there and I'm only making $8 an hour without commissions so I'm broke!" I can lean on that when I need it. I'm sure I'll need it about five times tonight. But I'll be Okay.

The mental fight between myself and my growling stomach during the time I'll be in and around fresh food being cooked will be the hardest. I'll have to fight the urge to pick off other people's' plates and try not to look hungry. What's the plan?

I'll excuse myself when the urge to pick off someone's plate, or when they offer becomes too much, or when they go to the bathroom. I'm sure I will end up doing this about nine times. Not because I have to go to the bathroom, but because it will be the only place, not in front of my new co-workers, where I can tell my stomach to "Shut up and stop growling!" Anyhow, tonight should be fun and getting my stomach to stop growling as waiters bring food around me is the least of my worries.

CHAPTER TWELVE
Starting to get a hold

CHAPTER TWELVE
Starting to get a hold

FINALLY DONE WITH MY SHOWER, and I'm now jumping out to get ready for tonight. I head over to my room, close the door behind me and peek into my closet at my three button down dress shirts that I've been wearing every other day to work and my one pair of pants. I ask myself, *I wonder what I'm going to wear tonight?* Decisions, decisions. Maybe I'll rip off the sleeves to one of my dress shirts and call it a "Muscle T button down shirt." But then again, my malnutrition ass would need muscles to make that a reality. Okay, never mind that idea.

The plan is simple. Be dressed and ready by the time they get here and meet them outside. Why? Because if they come up the stairs they're going to want to see my place, hang out and expect me to be a host. "Do you have any beer?" "No." "Can I get a glass of water?" "Yes, from the sink!" Never mind if they want to peek into my room unless that's all they want to see is an empty room with no bed, desk, dressers or TV. I do have a desktop computer on the

ground if they want to see that. So, the plan is to be ready and outside when they arrive and don't keep them waiting.
It's 8:15 p.m. and I'm ready, I'm also excited to be going out and doing something, anything, outside of just going to work and back. It's very cool. Add that to the fact that I'll be hanging out with some new potential friends since first becoming homeless and you have a recipe for a great night! It hits 8:25 p.m. and my phone goes off with a text. "What's your gate code again?" Nice! They're here and that's my cue to head downstairs. I text back "4226" as I'm locking my front door and heading down the stairs before they have a chance to park. I walk out towards the parking lot just as they come around the corner and turn into my parking area. I wave my hand as if they could see me, it's 8:30 at night and dark out. I really need to get this whole "going out with friend's thing" back on track. I wave again, this time in their headlights, as they pull up. I open the back passenger door to get in. There are two dudes in the back seat whom I don't know and two dudes in the front which I do know from work. I close the door and immediately the "What's ups?" come in from every angle.

"Hi! My name is Mike."
"Hi! My name is Joe."
"Hi! My name is David."

I'm thinking, '*Slow down, this is my first time in a long time*,' something that I used to hearing from girls back in the day when I had more muscles. I'm so excited to be on this play date with these guys right now that I won't remember any of their names immediately.

"Hey! I'm Holis!"

My co-worker places the car in drive and we are off. Our five-guy play date begins. The car isn't the only thing that takes off immediately, so do the conversations. The guy to my left asks, destination. An awesome spo"How do you know these guys up front?"

I say nervously, "From work!"

He nods. "Cool."

And just like that, I was in! With the entire sensory overload going on in the car I barely noticed that it was forty minutes later and that we have arrived at our t known to locals as the best place to grab microbrews, a.k.a. "expensive-ass-beers." We hop out of the car and make our way to the front doors. Once we step inside the bar, almost simultaneously as if we had just stepped out of a movie screen, we stare at the bar with our jaws on the floor. There are chicks everywhere! I haven't seen this many girls in on spot at the same time in a long time. A few seconds pass and one of the guys in our group brings us all back to reality.

"I guess we should find a spot to sit."

We find a nice little spot just off the bar next to the bathrooms. As soon as we sit the waitress comes over. In a comforting, light and airy southern voice she asks, "Hey y'all, what can I get you to start off with this evening?"

The guys start to order as if they've been here before. Probably have. Asking for beers I've never heard of.

Immediately I think, *Great! This will give me a real excuse to stare at the menu for the next fifteen minutes and in the meantime, sip on a glass of water with lemon.* The only thing I can afford, because it's free. She goes around the table, all the guys order, and I go last.

She asks me, "What are you getting, handsome?" She just called me 'Handsome', a tiny, little thrill goes through my body. I haven't heard a woman call me anything close to that in a very long time. I answer, "I have no idea, I've never been here before. Can I get a glass of water with lemon until I decide?" "Sure, no problem cutie." There it is again. She grabs all of the menus out of our hands except mine, and just as soon as I think that I'm home free and she's about to turn to walk away, one of the guys yells, "Wait! You know what? He'll take an Ugly Grandpa."

I think, *this guy, as nice as he is, just ordered me a drink and I have no way to pay for it!? What the fuck?*

I immediately jump in. "No, no, I don't like light beer."

He tries to reassure me quickly, "No, don't worry it's a dark."

She replies, "You got it!"

Fuck! I'm done. I'm history. How in the hell am I going to pay for this? This is *not* what I was expecting.
The beers come, and everyone starts to drink. I don't drink mine. I stare at it. I'm thinking to myself, *how can I get out of paying for this? I can tell her that the beer is flat? No, she'll just bring me a new one.* Geez, how the heck did this happen? One of the guys says, "What? He gets you an Ugly Grandpa and you're not going to toast him?" I look up and everyone has their drinks in the air. Fuck it. I'm all in at this point. We cheer, and I drink. Kitchen duty, here I come. We finish them and without warning, the next round comes. All of us get the same exact drinks that we had for the first round. This waitress is good, but she's secretly becoming my worst enemy.

Doing her job, she keeps bringing me beers I can't pay for. I can't pay for these, so I don't dare to take a sip out of this one. I should do something, or this is going to continue, and I have zero dollars to my name. Nothing in my back pocket, nothing in my wallet, nothing anywhere on me. I lean over to my co-worker and nod for him to lean in. He does.

I whisper, "Bro, I have no idea how I'm going to pay for these. I don't have any money. I've only been at our job for three weeks and, unlike you, I'm not making any commissions yet."

There's my line, my ace in the hole has been used. The line I would use to defend my choice of getting just a water with lemon in it instead of a beer.

He just shrugs it off and whispers, "Don't worry bro, I invited you out, and besides, we've all been there. You're going to broke for the first ninety days until they decide to put you on commission scale, so get used to it."

If he only knew how 'Used to it' I was. Why? Why would this guy do this for me? He barely even knows me. And did he just say ninety days? That's not what I was told in my interview. He taps me on the shoulder and says, "So don't worry, I got you. Now, can you stop whispering in my ear like a fourteen-year-old schoolgirl and let me get back to my beer please?" I thank him and gladly let him get back to his beer. My new-found friend and I have an understanding. He has my back and from this point on, I officially have his. I'll cheers to that with this second beer any day.

About a million jokes, forty-two laughs and three hours later we finish up. My new friend pays for my beers and we head out. He's awesome! The car ride back to my place was grand. Cracking jokes in the car. Talking about female celebrities that we would sleep with if we ever met them on the street (as if they would sleep with us?). We get to my community. I give them the gate code and we make our way to my building. Just as we were about to pull up into my building and right before I'm about to get out Dave yells out, "Man, I have to piss like a racehorse!"

I pretend to not hear him. He looks and pokes me in the shoulder. "Dude, you gotta let me up to use your bathroom like right now!" Great. This was exactly what I was trying to avoid at the top of the night.

We've been out all night. We've had a great time drinking and now I'm going to be the guy that says, "No, you can't come up into my house to use my toilet"? After their friend, my co-worker, paid for my drinks all night? Hesitantly, I say, "Okay, but you better be quick, I have to work in the morning." As in, "You're going straight to my bathroom and don't expect a tour, either."

He says, "Yeah, for sure."

Next thing I know, like Christmas lights they all start to light up. "You know what? I got to pee really bad too, bro!" "I go to go too, bro." and "So do I!" started coming out of everyone's mouths in the car. Reluctantly, once again I say, "Okay, guys, come on up but everyone must be quick! My roommate is asleep." We all get out of the car and head up to my place. We head up the stairs. I open my front door and turn on the lights. Immediately the compliments pour in. "Dude, this is a nice place!" "This is a pimp pad." And so on. I nervously say "Yeah, thanks. Anyhow, the bathroom is down there." I point down the hall. "The first door on your left," as if to say, "Let's hurry this up." The guys remaining start to make their way around my condo in all different directions. Giving themselves a tour.

"Is this your kitchen?"

I make my way to the kitchen. "Yes, it is."

"Is this your balcony?"

I make my way over to the balcony "Yes, it is".

Then from behind me I hear it, "Who's room is this?"

I look back and the door to my room has been opened and I reluctantly reply in an ashamed childlike voice, "This, this is my room."

Silence.

Then, finally Joe tries to break the silence with a witty comment. "No, seriously, who's room is this?"

Again, I say, "It's my room."

Then it starts. "For real. You sleep in here?" "What's with the computer on the floor and where's your bed?" "How come you don't have any clothes in your closet?" "No TV?" "What's with the one sheet on the floor?" "Dude, you're not broke, you're dirt poor!"

I'm embarrassed…as if I had just begged all of them for a $1 from a street corner. My co-worker looks at me as if to say, "Now I know why you didn't have any money to pay for your drinks tonight." A flush comes from the bathroom. A door opens, and David makes his way out of the bathroom, down the hall and into my room. The weird tension and silence is obvious.

David asks cheerfully, "What did I miss?"
My co-worker says, "Nothing, let's go."

David is puzzled. "I thought you guys had to go to the bathroom, too?"

My co-worker grunts, "We don't have to go anymore. Let's go."

They all make their way to the front door. Walk out. And I lock the door behind them. I don't know if my co-worker wanted to leave because he felt bad for me, or if he felt like I lied to him. I don't know if it would have been better for me to be honest. Would it have been better to say that I couldn't pay for my drinks because I'm just now getting back on my feet after recently being homeless? No matter what, what's done is done and you can bet this would be the last time I ever have anyone over every again. Period.

What seems like nothing in their eyes is everything to me. I have a roof over my head, I have four walls, I have security, and I'm not outside dealing with the elements. I have a shower, I have cabinets that I can put food in and I have a shower, cable TV, security, and warmth. *I have everything!*

But hey…maybe they're right. Without knowing my story why would they think that? Why would anyone? In their eyes, I was not up to or anywhere near their level and I wasn't worth hanging out with. Especially after tonight. I head back to my room, head down. I turn the light off and pass out on my floor. I've had enough of this for one night.

It's about four in the morning when I wake up. I am wide awake. I'm still irritated at what my co-worker said. It's not his fault. They have no idea what my story is or how far I've come so far.

How would they have known if I didn't come out and tell them? I get up, turn the light on, sit up on my floor and stare into my mirrored closet doors. Now, it's plainly obvious that I'm not going back to sleep.

To pass the time I start staring at the guy in the mirror. I use this time to start asking myself some serious questions. I say, "You're up, you can't sleep, and you obviously have a lot more work to do in your life. You have a lot more self-improvement work to do and after knowing this, what are you going to do?" There was no answer but there was a sudden urge to go outside and to go for a walk. "I'm going to go walking, that's what I'm going to do" Is my reply to myself. Sounded like a pretty good answer at the time and yes, I know this doesn't solve anything but, it felt good to decide and to be doing outside of my room about it.
Keep in mind, I know that I'm not up to anyone's standards, which is why I haven't spoken to any girls or tried dating. I'm more pissed at myself than my

co-workers because their comments just reminded me of how much farther I must go.

Yes, I've come far but not far enough. I get up, grab a pair of my work pants, a button down and prepare to go walking.

Not much for walking gear but still, I'm going to be doing something with this time I have on my hands right now and I could care less that it's four in the morning. I hit the door. I walk down the stairs and make my way towards the entrance to my community. I walk out the large iron gates and make a left. Why a left? I have no idea, it just felt good to do so. After about forty-five feet that voice starts to creep in.

You know that voice, that voice that somehow always finds a way to creep in just as you're about to be something and starts to undermine you with, "What are you doing? You can't do this. You're no good at this." Yep, that voice. That voice that says you will never amount to anything, that same voice is telling me right now, 'It's four o'clock in the morning. You look like a moron out here walking in your work clothes, in the dark. Why don't you go home and cry about it? Go back to sleep on your floor, you look stupid you poor bastard. Everything won't be okay in the morning but at least you've gotten to sleep on it."

Now, this would be the moment where most people, including my old self, would turn around and go, "You're right, Voice in my head. I am a loser and yes, it is too early in the morning to be doing this. I do look like a moron out here walking at four in the morning." But not this time! This time I don't turn around, this time the voice in my head doesn't win and only starts to piss me off even more! By now I'm fuming. Instead of turning around, I find myself stepping harder, moving forward with every step, and walking stronger with every stride. Next thing I know, I'm walking fast, almost jogging, and getting farther and farther down the road. I'm far from my house now, I can feel it. The sun is coming up and I'm about fifteen minutes from my house before I decided I should stop and check where I'm at. I stop at the next intersection and look up at the cross-street signs. Flamingo & Hualapai? How the heck did I get all the way out here? There is no way I just walked fifty minutes? I take a seat on top of a big rock just off to the side at the intersection. I need to rest a bit. I'm sure that the people passing me by on their way to work are thinking, "Sucks to be that guy, walking to work." What they failed to notice was that I wasn't walking towards a job, *I was walking towards a breakthrough.*

I realized a few things in my pissed off walk this morning.

Number One: When that fire is burning inside of me, like when I'm pissed off and motivated, I can push myself much further than I ever thought possible. Number Two: That with will, drive and determination that I can shut down that stupid voice up inside my head that tells me that "I'm not good enough". Not only shut it down, but completely silence it all together. Even if it's just for a moment! And Number Three: I kind of like this four in the morning walking stuff! Yeah, it was early, but it was also silent. My phone wasn't ringing, I wasn't responding back to text messages and I can sit out here alone with my thoughts, quietly. It was almost therapeutic, relaxing and thoughtful all at the same time.

It was almost as if the world has shut down, closed its doors just for me and my thoughts. I felt lifted and the stress itself was off my shoulders. Without even knowing it yet, I had proven to myself that I'm stronger than I give myself credit for. Isn't that the story with all of us? I get up and I decide that no matter what's going on, I'm going to get up every morning and take a walk at six. Five days a week, Monday through Friday. Walk as far as I like and come back. It doesn't have to be fifteen miles, it could be fifteen feet, it doesn't matter, if I do something. What matters is that I'm out of bed, shutting down that negative inner voice, and I'm doing something to better myself. Mentally and physically.

I've made myself a promise to do this. I turn, take my first step and start to make my walk back home. As I walk back my next thought sneaks in. *Boy do my feet hurt and if I'm going to be doing this every morning, I'd better get myself another set of shoes, pronto.*

CHAPTER THIRTEEN
Decisions and habits

CHAPTER THIRTEEN
Decisions and habits

NEXT DAY. It's about seven thirty in the morning and it is safe to say, I didn't take that walk I promised myself yesterday. I promised myself that I would start walking every morning at six in the morning. Not just for exercise, but to get in the routine of starting my day off on the right foot and with a clear mind. To be honest, my feet still hurt from yesterday's fifty-minute walk, but deep down, I know that's just an excuse. It's hard to make life changes...Wait, that was an excuse, too. It's not hard to make life changes. What *is* hard is doing what you say you're going to do. Keeping yourself accountable, that's hard. What really happened was that I woke up around the same time as usual, but I woke up without the fire I had yesterday to get me up and take that walk I committed to yesterday. That's the truth. And the excuses end today.

I need to make this decision today, right now, because if I don't make the decision to do something about missing my walk this morning, then I never will. Decision means to 'Cut off' or 'Start anew', and that's exactly what I plan to do.

Besides, I'm doing this for me and if I don't do this for me, then who else will? I'm not going to let lack of motivation get in the way of what I want. I truly want to wake up at six in the morning and take a fifteen-mile walk; I do! Why? Because I can, and because it's challenging. Not to mention, I could probably use the exercise. I lost some weight thanks to not eating and no beer drinking, but that doesn't mean that I'm in shape. Going homeless has a way of doing that to you. I'm determined, and this walk will happen today! I'll try and shoot for three p.m. No! I'm going to do it at three p.m. Consider it done.

I've also decided today that I'm going to reach out to my ex for the first time in months. I've been building excuses there, too. I haven't tried calling or seeing my son since the day we were evicted. Partly because I was embarrassed and because I was ashamed of being such a failure in her eyes. The day we were evicted my ex made sure her and my son had a place to go. What can I say? She was a smart girl. Even when everything was falling apart around us she still had the foresight to plan and make sure that she and my son had a safe place to go. Every day she was coming home from work with printouts of condos for rent near her job. I secretly was hoping that she was planning our plan B while I worked on plan A. That wasn't the case.

The day of our eviction as we sat on the sidewalk just a few feet from where our old stuff was being thrown out, she told me that she was going left and that I should go right. I knew what she meant, but my heart didn't want to believe it. She was saying, in her way, that we were separating, that our family was breaking up, and that I was not invited in the direction that they were going in. I guess I should have seen it coming. I had done too little to mend our past and too much wrong to move forward into the future with them. There's a certain point when you continue to do wrong by your partner and not learn from your mistakes as a partner, there is no getting them back once they decide you are a waste of their time now. As I sit with my thoughts, I also wonder what my son is doing right now as I write this. I wonder if he still remembers me. I wonder how tall he is. If he's speaking yet…I wonder.

I wonder if I call if my ex will she even answer the phone or, more likely, will she throw me straight into her voice mail? She might not even have the same

number. On the other hand, what if she answers, what will she say? What will I say? Will she have forgiven me for all the wrong choices I've made? Would she be holding a grudge? Will she curse me out? Will she be worried for me? Will she even want to speak to me? I don't know.
To have any one of those questions above actually answered can be scary all by itself. But, it is time to push those excuses to the side and suck it up, because when it comes to my son, I need to see how *he* is doing. I need to see him. Right now, I have nothing to offer him. I know that, but I do have a voice over the phone that I can offer for now and I hope that's enough. We can at least pick up where we left off and I could get him familiar with my voice again. You know what? Enough questions, enough procrastinating, where's my phone? I'm calling her now!

I grab my phone and find her number in my contracts and press dial. It's too late to turn back now, the phone is dialing, and it is ringing on her end. Palms start to become sweaty, there are thoughts of becoming nervous. What if she answers? It has easily been months since I've spoken to them both. Five rings and no answer, I receive her voice mail. I wipe the sweat off my hands on my pants and continue to leave a message. "Hey, It's me. I was wondering how you guys were doing. I'm fine. I have a roof over my head. I've been here for a couple of weeks now. I don't know if you ever want to talk to me again and if you don't, I completely understand, but I do want to know how my son is doing. I wanted to know if I could see him soon. My phone, miraculously, is still on so you can text me if you want. Even if you hate me, just call, so that I know you guys are okay. Thanks." I hang up.

I don't think she will call me back and if she does, it's to tell me how much she hates me and how much I fucked up. I get it and I did and some part of me knows that I deserve it. I'm sure the word 'Loser' will come out about fifteen times before we can even start talking about my son. It is something I know I absolutely must go through to be able to finally start talking about my son. So, I will grin and bear it, just as if nothing has changed and we're back in our old condo; still together and still fighting. It's kind of like re-opening a bad scab, hoping that once the scab heals after being re-opened, it will heal that much stronger. At least, that's what I tell myself.

It's Sunday and there's no return phone call from my ex or a text. Go figure. I do wonder how my mom is doing, and since I'm in the mood of making life decisions, I call her too. I miss my mom and I miss my grandmother. My grandmother is the best. For the longest I can remember, she was a high school teacher who taught tenth and twelfth grade level English courses. She was known for her red pen and correcting her students' tests at the dinner table in her kitchen. She would also constantly correct all family members who spoke English incorrectly in her house. Regarding her red pen, it was also not unusual to see her in the kitchen after dinner grading papers from her students with it. I would watch her and try to figure out why some students would receive an F and others would receive an A. Even to this day she's never told me. Like a true teacher, she always wanted me to figure it out for myself. What I remember the most is how she would scream corrections in our grammar throughout the house when we would visit. "Excuse me, but *ain't* is not a word!" was the most familiar comment that came from my grandmother. Being kids, specifically brothers and sisters, we were always butchering the English language and constantly trying to create our own slang. At any given time, you could hear my grandmother correcting us from the kitchen upstairs while we are in the den downstairs. She was always quick with the corrections, with or without her red pen.

My grandfather passed earlier this year and she has been spending a lot of time with my mom at her house. I know if I call, she and my mom will be there. I call, there is no answer. I leave a voicemail. No surprise, it's been around the same amount of time since I've called back home and spoken to her and my grandmother, so she wouldn't be expecting my call. Plus, it's Sunday which means my mom is probably in the City (New York City), treating my grandmother to a nice dinner. It's kind of a ritual for them both and they love it. To be honest, I don't know how I would answer her if she was to ask, "What have you been up to? Are you OK?" I wouldn't be able to hold back from breaking down halfway through my answers if she did ask. I switch gears and then proceed to call my brothers and my sister. No one answers there either. I leave voicemails letting everyone know that I am fine, even though they have no idea of what I've been going through. I leave messages. "Hey, I'm alive! You can call off the search and give me a call me back when you get this. Love you!" I thought it was not only fitting but quirky. As I was making my calls, though, I can't help but feel an overwhelming idea. *Why can't I do this every Sunday? You know what? I 'm going to make this a habit too! I'm going to call back home every Sunday!* And that is exactly what I'm going to do.

Every Sunday like clockwork I call home. Nothing else matters. Sunday is calling day. I use this day to rebuild my connection with my mom, my grandmother, my brothers and my sister, my family and my friends. Sunday is not for work or worries anymore, Sunday is now for family. During this, I've also decided I'm not waiting for three o'clock to go on my walk. I'm going for my walk right now and that's exactly what I do. It takes me about three hours to do one round trip. Not bad for my first walk, well, technically second. I'll get better.

With every day that I get up to do my five miles walk I become stronger. I can't help but think to myself that there must be a better way to get the exercise I'm searching for in a reasonable amount of time without having to take three hours out of my day to get it. A bike, maybe? Why not? I'm beginning to love the outdoors again, but this three-hour round-trip dedication to exercise will also become too time consuming as I get busier with my new goals, especially, if I want to seriously start doing this daily. That question will have to wait. I'm exhausted; I need to shower and get to bed (get to sleeping on the ground on a sheet), and tomorrow is Monday and that means it's back to work.

Monday comes, and I had to deal with the co-workers from Friday night. The same ones that came to my place and saw that I was sleeping on the floor in my own room. They made it easy for me, though. They don't communicate with me at all, just a quick "'Sup" in the morning when they come in. Since my desk is the first desk you walk by when you come into the office, it's kind of hard to pass by me without saying anything. If they did, that would have been straight disrespectful, and I don't think they would have meant that. To be honest, who cares? I'm way past caring what people say or think of me. I'm a new man on a new mission.

It is what it is. I'm more excited about this Friday because it's payday! It's the week I get a whole $330 bucks for putting in close to forty-seven hours last week! I've been working hard to impress my boss and been putting in some overtime. They don't pay for overtime but, my work ethic of being the first one in the office and the last one to leave the office is something that is embedded in my DNA that I can't get rid of. Plus, I've showed them that I'm willing to pay the price if they are willing to put me on commission scale sooner than later.

I'm really excited this week, too, because this is also the week where I pay off my ride share! Miss Puerto Rico will be getting her $300 out of my paycheck and I get a whole thirty bucks! Back in the day, I used to pay thirty bucks to the valet alone just to park my car. Today it's a different story. I see that same thirty dollars in a different way than I used to, and I'm proud of that. After picking up pennies off the ground and collecting enough of them to roll up fifty cents so that I can purchase a travel size bag of Doritos for dinner, you would look at thirty bucks a whole lot differently, too! Dare I say it? Payday Friday! *I'm going to be rich!* I'm going to visit the Dollar Store and fill up my cabinets with fifteen buck's worth of food! Spaghetti, spaghetti sauce, bread, peanut butter and jelly, you name it! The remaining fifteen? I'll take some of that and take my son out somewhere awesome this weekend. Maybe Pizza Play. He loves that place. I can cash in a five-dollar bill for quarters and hold him in my lap as he plays video games all day long there and I will absolutely love it! I can also do McDonald's. I can get him not one, but two forty-nine-cent ice cream cones and let him play in the McDonald's playground with the other kids for hours on end for free! It's a win for everyone. Hey, I know it's not exactly a lot, but it's a plan. Granted, of course, if his mom calls me back.

I know I've made a lot of promises to myself and that's okay. As a matter of fact, I don't look at them as promises anymore. I look at them as decisions now. Promises you can always break or back out of, but decisions you must stand behind.

I'm making decisions today, building blocks if you will, that will lead to, form and create amazing habits, habits that will ultimately make me a person who I've always imagined myself to be.

A more complete person who not only inspires but is inspiring to be around and it all starts with one promise—sorry, one decision—to do one thing different for myself that I did not do yesterday to get me to where I need to be tomorrow. Yeah, I've made a lot of decisions to change my life, but hey, if not me then who else? And to be honest, I was never a fan of hitting the ground crawling, or a fan of making excuses. At least, not anymore.

CHAPTER FOURTEEN
The call

CHAPTER FOURTEEN
The call

MY PHONE IS AT MY EAR. There is no noise on the line. It's completely silent.

My ex has just called. It's the first time she's called me since our eviction out of our old condo. I answer, and I just say, "Hello?" A couple of seconds go by. Nothing. I say, "Hello?" again. I'm thinking that maybe her phone called me by mistake? Before I could finish that thought and hang up she replies, "So, you're alive?"

It's official, nope, her phone *did not* just call me by accident. I amazingly muster up enough courage to say, "Yeah." There is no way this moment is happening right now. I'm asking myself, *Is this real? Am I really on the phone right now with me ex?* and not because I miss her, but because she is the only person on the planet right now that would have any idea of what I have been going through, what we've gone through.

Numerous feelings start to overcome me. Feelings of joy, feelings of love, thoughts of loss, and thoughts of the good times, then those feelings and thoughts turn to bad memories and high anxiety. Argh. I'm starting to remember how our relationship ended and I know sooner than later this call is going to go wrong. There is too much pain there for this to be a pleasant phone call for too long. The feelings become overwhelming and I want to break down, but I can't. I don't

want to be completely open or that vulnerable with her just yet. I don't know where her head is at or why she's calling and I'm not going to give her that satisfaction if she isn't calling with good intentions. Breaking down in front of her at this moment is not an option. I want to tell her that it's been rough. That I've been eating out of garbage cans. That I have been sleeping on the floor on the ground. That I've been homeless and haven't been eating. I have been happy that I have security, a roof over my head, a room (even though I don't have a bed in it) and I a little bit of food in my cabinets. I want to talk about how happy I am to have a job and to have an income even though it's just eight bucks an hour and that I have some money saved up for my son, although it's not a lot. But I don't tell her. Not yet. This call is still surreal, and I know that deep down it's going to go bad, quickly. I know I shouldn't think this way but it's true. Our relationship, if you want to call it that, is a lot like eating Sour Patch Kids. First, they're sour, then they're sweet, but with her, she's the complete opposite. First, she's sweet then she's sour, I mean really, really, sour. At least with me.

Her next question comes. "What have you been doing?" I tell her. I tell her what I did the day of the eviction and what I did after the days that followed. About sleeping in Eric's abandoned office and after months of being homeless that I finally found a room for rent and a job.

I don't get too deep into the conversation though, I'm still waiting to see where her head is at. I must admit, I'm liking the fact that we're casually speaking right now. Being civil...And, *boom!* goes the dynamite. I spoke too soon. We've been on the phone talking happily for a good seven or ten minutes—which is a record for us—and yep, just as I suggested, it isn't long before she moves the conversation into how much of a fuck up I am. How I got us evicted and how irresponsible I am. How I'm a complete 'Loser' and how my son probably won't remember me because I'm a piece of shit. My immediate thought, *Really, you're going to go there?* my son *not remembering me? That's a low blow, even for you.*

The call now starts to turn negative and very angry very fast. It's not long before she starts the name calling. She starts to yell. Whenever she gets upset or drunk, her voice goes up two octaves, right now it's at a nine. She's really pissed. She starts to get *me* upset and defensive. "You're such a loser." "You couldn't be more of a piece of shit." We're going nowhere. We need to calm down. I try to switch the conversation back to something positive.

I ask, "How's my son? Where is he?"
Still angry, she replied, "He's right here."
I ask as nicely as I can, "Can you put me on speaker phone, so I can talk to him?"
She scoffs, "For what? He won't remember you."
In my head I want to scream, are *you fucking kidding me?* Instead, I say, "I would like to talk to him, please!"

She snaps, "No."

Now I'm getting pissed, again.

Before I say something, I don't mean, I mentally take a step back. I get myself together. I try to calm down. Let's make this right. Let me start from the beginning and hope that this makes a difference in the conversation and ultimately allows me to speak to my son. I take 100% responsibility and apologize for getting us evicted. I apologize for being irresponsible with my decisions, wasteful with my choices, and her heart. I apologize for not putting her first. I apologize for every lie I ever told and for cheating on her in the beginning of our relationship six years ago. I apologize for everything and anything *and* I mean it! Honestly and wholeheartedly.

She calms down, sort of. Her voice comes one octave. The name calling doesn't stop, but at least she's calmer now. I get it, she's hurt. She's embarrassed for the eviction. She's angry. She trusted me, and I failed. I get it, but I don't want her to put what I did to our relationship's past or what I did to her get in between me and my son. I really want to talk to him, but it soon becomes clear that I'm not going to be speaking to my lil' man today. Not on this call.

So, I let her go. I've had enough name calling being thrown at me on this call to last the next lifetime. It's safe to say that some things don't change.

I ask one last time, "When can I see him?"

She replies forcefully, "When you become a real man."

I can only say, "Understood. I'll talk to you later."

I hang up. Beaten up and broken down. I feel like, with bare hands that I've just gone to battle with a raging pissed off two-ton bull. I survived but, I have absolutely no energy. No more energy to keep writing. Plus, it's hard to write with tears hitting the paper beneath me. I don't feel like writing anymore. Talk to you later journal.

It's the next day. I've put yesterday's call behind me and it's back to work as usual. It's me back to killing it as usual. I'm finally back to normal. That call yesterday took a lot out of me. I don't know if it's me or natural talent or just the new idea in my head that nothing can stop me and that I will never go back to being homeless ever again that's driving me, but I've booked two moves this morning and have decided to talk to the boss about finally being able to collect commissions. I think I've proven myself so far. I know I have not been here ninety days yet, but he has got to see the hard work I'm putting in and has to know that I am serious about making some real money. This is the moment I've been working so hard for. I want to make sure I have a leg to stand on when we have this conversation and by the looks of my sales, he might have to give me his legs. It's around 10:40 a.m. I walk over to his desk, ask if I can speak to him and I pull him to the side. It is twenty minutes before he takes his famous hour-long lunch. I want to catch him before he comes back from lunch full and tired and counting the minutes before it's five p.m. and time to go home.

I ask him if he's happy with my production.

He says, "Yes!"
I then ask, "When can I expect to go on commission plus an hourly?"

He says without hesitation, "Right now!"

I'm a little shocked. "Wait,
He smiles, "I was going to pull *you* aside and tell you that I'm putting you on salary plus commission as of today. Everything that you have made up to this point is not commissionable, but everything you make from this day forward will be!"

I just want to be clear. "Does that include the moves I booked this morning?"

He pauses and says, "Let me think about it, but again as of right now, you will have your commissions."

I'm dancing inside. I ask him what the commission percentage was again. He says, "Ten percent."

I tell him that I want twelve percent.

He looks at me like I'm crazy.

I insist, "You know I'm good for it. I won't tell anyone in the office and if you give me that twelve percent, I'll give you an additional fifty thousand in moves by this time next month."

The craziness that was on his face is now replaced with a smile.

He says, "Fifty thousand? You're going to do an additional fifty thousand in moves by this time next month? Really?" I'm confident, "Yes! And if I don't make it, you can drop me down to ten and we'll act as if we never had this conversation. But when I do hit fifty grand in additional moves, you owe me twelve percent commission plus salary what?" on fifty thousand dollars in moves."

He says, "Let me think about it." He congratulates me, and we return to the office and back onto the sales floor. I know he's going to say yes. That additional fifty grand would make our office number one in the company and I know his ego would want him to at least try. Like I've said before, he's a sales rep turned accidental manager. He would not allow me to not at least try. The bad news is that if he says yes, which I know he will, that I will have to work even harder than I've ever worked here prior. But that's okay. I'm game.

I'm ready. I've done about thirty-two thousand in moves so far and adding an additional fifty grand would mean that by this time next month I would have had to make and surpass eighty-two thousand dollars in moves! It's a tall order to deliver, but I'm up for it. I head back to my desk and immediately go to work. I grab for my "Maybe" folder and start making some calls.

This "Maybe" folder is full of people who I've called or who have called in that I've pitched, and they said just that: "Maybe." I try not to keep leads in this folder for too long. If I've haven't spoken to them in two days or less I let them go or give the lead to another sales rep. I don't sweat the leads. I know there will be more and usually after two days they have picked another mover or have gone stale. And it's on to the next one for me. But, in between today and two days from now, it's game on. I start making calls to everyone in my "Maybe" folder that's fallen in that two-day timeline.

The first guy says, "We've found someone locally to move us, but thanks."

The next one, "We've decided to move ourselves with a U-Haul."

The Next," We've chosen another national mover."

Geez, I know there's a move in here somewhere, I can feel it. Fourth guy, no answer. Fifth guy, voice mail. Sixth guy, Bingo*!* Booked him for a move. Houston, Texas to Miami, Florida with a drop-off in Orlando. He's dropping off a few couches to his son's house in Orlando. $8,599, plus tax. I just made a commission! On a $8,599 move at twelve percent commission, that's $1,031.88. Who's the man?

At just ten percent that would have been a $859 commission. Yeah, it's okay money but it's amazing what an additional two percent will bring you. The rest of the day is kind of slow as far as sales go. No moves booked in the afternoon, but I'm still riding high. It's slowly approaching five p.m. I think today I will leave on time, as in the time I'm supposed to leave, the office shuts down at five and the rest of the other employees leave. Even though I usually don't leave until six or seven, I deserve it. Today I feel like I've accomplished a lot for just ten hours of work. No need to work thirteen today. I shutdown my computer and as I'm making my way to the front door, I hear my boss yell, "Holis!"

I stop and answer, "Yes?"

He says, "Good job booking that move this morning and your answer is Yes. You can have it!" A smile comes to my face. I already knew I had it, but I needed that confirmation. I reply," Yes, sir, thank you, sir!" It's amazing. Confirmation that I am on the right track. That I am doing something positive in my life. I'm making decisions. Taking a stand and making the right changes. Working hard and getting what you want is a good feeling, too. I exit the office and I head outside to see if Kent is here yet. He is Miss Puerto Rico's boyfriend. Besides a call from my ex, his negativity is the only thing that can bring me off my high horse. Not today though. It would take ten phone calls from my ex and nineteen car rides with Kent all back to back to kill my stride today. Today, I'm the man! I get outside, what a surprise, he's not here. I wish you could hear the sarcasm.

He started picking me up last week and I left my desk at exactly 5pm, it is now 5:30. At 5:45 and after five text messages later, without any response back, he finally shows up, late, again. There is nothing fast about this guy and when he is in the room, his personality is that everyone should feel blessed that he is even in the room with us. I knew this was going to start happening. I called it last week on Friday when I didn't give him the extra fifty bucks a week he demanded for his own back pocket. Not to mention, he said nothing about giving Miss Puerto Rico any of it. I knew he was going to start pulling stuff like this.

He's in his work truck. I get in. I don't say much. He does enough talking and bashing for the both of us. Again, he's going off on how Miss Puerto Rico's kids aren't his and how much of a saint he is because he's willing to date a single mom with four kids. Argh. This guy is a big time piece of shit.

My mom was a single mom with five kids who worked her ass off to make sure we had a roof over our head and to make sure we were fed, I can't help but imagine that what he says is probably the same thing those other guys who dated my mom when I was younger would say behind her back. I think to myself, wishing I could say to him, *every day that you wake up next to her you're choosing to be with her, you moron. Obviously, there is something you like about her enough that keeps you around every day. If you're that much of a Saint and can't stand her, leave! But don't talk shit behind her back about a hard-working single mother or her four kids.*

Then again, maybe I shouldn't throw stones. I've never talked crap about my ex, *ever*, but maybe I should shut up now. I did date my ex for six years, five of which were horrific, (I'm talking responsibility for this by the way) and I didn't leave. So, yep! I'm not a hypocrite so keeping my thoughts to myself sounds like a good idea right about now.

Finally, I'm home. He drops me off and I head upstairs. Time for my five-star dining experience of spaghetti and toast, my meal for the evening. Nonetheless, I'm excited about putting together a plan to meet and exceed that additional fifty grand in moves I promised my boss earlier today. This means working seven a.m. to seven p.m. Monday through Friday. It means volunteering for Saturdays— Saturdays are commission only days, no salary—and even a few hours on Sundays, which are, again, commission only, but only after I call back home first.

It means going back to all my happy moves prior and hitting them up for referrals and recommendations, which will come in handy as a marketing angle for more moves. This ultimately means long days and even longer nights with no days off. I don't care. Plus, I've been through worse and if my boss delivers what he's promised—because I know I will—then of course, I'm game. If he doesn't deliver, then he better get ready to meet hells fire.

CHAPTER FIFTEEN
Pissed the fuck off

CHAPTER FIFTEEN
Pissed the fuck off

IT'S BEEN AWHILE SINCE I'VE WRITTEN IN MY JOURNAL, but that's only because I have been killing it at work. I'm sorry, journal, but I have missed you!

It's full steam ahead. My plan has been set in place at work all week, with being the first one in and the last one out of the office. Nothing unusual there, but the only thing that has changed is when five p.m. rolls around and everyone else is shutting down their computers and leaving, I'm still on the phone booking moves. My attitude is, "See you later, slackers,'" as I still answer the phone and take calls way after five p.m., Pacific Standard Time. Unlike these guys, I promised my boss an extra $50,000 in moves this month and that doesn't happen by clocking out at five and calling it a day.

Plus, in the after hours, I get to tweak and perfect my pitch. I get to try new things and find what works and what doesn't work, all while not having to worry about any of the other reps hearing my flow and attempting to steal it from me.

Don't get me wrong, it's not like I'm selling vacuums over the phone, or the cure for toe fungus, but these are people who are moving are calling because they need guidance. At least, that's the way I see it. Now, I don't know if you've ever moved cross country before, but it's a pain in the butt. I moved and drove myself from Jersey to Vegas and it was horrifying. I drove basically non-stop, only stopping within the first twelve hours. I slept for four hours at that stop and continued to drive the remainder of my trip straight through. It was a huge pain in the ass; literally, sitting on your butt for forty-two hours straight is never fun. It's such a pain that I vowed to never take that trip ever again, at least by car.

Even though many people move for many different reasons, most of the people I deal with here at work are moving for either for a new job or for personal reasons. They're moving to be closer to family or their new job. It's not like they're moving across the street either, they're making long distance moves, so I can relate. Los Angeles to New York City, or New York City to Washington State. This happens daily and it's happening whether they like it or not, and they're going to be moving *with someone* and who better to move them, *than me*?

I'm the best at what I do because I can relate and because I have their best interest in mind. To make sure their move will never be as hard as mine was. So, I'm killing it. I'm not just applying a great work ethic, but I'm also under-promising and over-delivering. I'm taking my moves very seriously, like if it was my move all over again.

I've been doing some company no-no's, like giving out my personal cell phone number and my personal email address to customers. I've been delivering exceptional customer service and doing exactly what I say I would to do for every client, on every move. Even if I didn't promise it originally, or if there were changes in shipment, changes in their moving dates, or charged for last-minute stops, where other reps in the office would have given up and said "No", I said "No" also. "No problem!" and I made it happen, within guidelines, whatever it took.

I cannot tell you how many calls I've taken this week after nine pm at night from west coast customers calling for quotes after work and after dinner. I've taken calls as late as eleven at night, and as early as three in the morning from east coast customers calling to get a moving quote before work. I'm taking complaint calls while in bed from customers ranging from late deliveries to the drivers getting lost, from the drivers themselves complaining that they cannot find the customer's address. I've even taken calls from the laborers complaining that there are too many stairs, too many floors and underestimated weight values.

The list goes on. I cannot tell you how many times I've had a customer call me on my cell phone and keep me up all night long complaining about their final bill. Comes with the territory of giving out your cell phone number to customers, but it also pays off in the end because the customers will know that I am there for them 24/7, even after the doors close for the day.

With this approach, what I found is that in the end the customers are absolutely thrilled and usually cannot wait to give me referrals for others who are also moving. I even hear compliments such as, "If I ever move again it will definitely be with you!" "I'm going to tell all my friends about you!"

The whole time all I want to do is get back to sleep. Don't get me wrong, I love the fact that I am able to deliver for them, but these moves do tend to take their toll when your customers have direct access to you 24/7. No complaints here, just another day and night in the life of Mr. Holis, long distance mover extraordinaire who gives his cell phone number out to his customers. Maybe now I can finally get some sleep. Somebody must be up at six in the morning for their fifteen-mile walk. Then shower, then breakfast then out the door for work.

A nap and two hours later, I take my walk and end up keeping the promise I made to myself that I would take these walks every morning, Monday through Friday. Sometimes I take fifteen-minute walks and sometimes I take a six-mile walk. No matter what, if it's raining, if I don't feel like it, it doesn't matter, every morning I'm walking. I get back just in time to take a shower, get dressed, grab a bowl and a package of Ramen Noodles for lunch and head outside to meet Kent. It's dark, it's about 6:30 in the morning, around the time Kent should be here waiting for me outside. I rush downstairs and out to the parking lot and of course, he's not there. Where the heck is he? I need to be at work in a half hour. Just as I'm about to open my phone and send him a text message asking him where he is, I begin to see headlights from behind building Number Two in my apartment community approaching. I secretly pray, *please be him.*

It is. Thank god. He pulls up. I get in and we're off. Looks like I'll be on time for work after all, even if I only had two hours of sleep.

Now, I can't tell you what the conversation was with him this morning because to be honest, I was still sleeping, even after my brisk walk. Honestly, by now I've just stopped listening. I might be in the car physically, but mentally I'm somewhere else. He never has anything positive to say anyway about Miss Puerto Rico or even life in general, and if he wasn't my rideshare to and from work, I wouldn't even be associated with him. I don't do drama. I don't talk about people behind their backs. I'm not one for paying attention to rumors, so I've learned to shut him out. He might be my ride to and from work, but he is not my friend.

No matter how tired I am from not sleeping, and all of Kent's rambling nonsense, all of that should come to an end now because I can see my job's parking lot coming up in the near distance. I must get serious. Yesterday was just another day and today is a new day. Rain or shine I promised my boss an extra $50,000 in moves this month, so I leave Kent's truck quickly to run up the stairs to my building and get to my desk.

I drop my bag down on my chair, and just as I start to turn on my computer my cell phone rings. My first thoughts are, *it must be Kent. What does he want now?* I pick up my phone and look at the caller I.D. to see who's calling. To my surprise, it's not Kent, it's my ex. *It's seven a.m. There must be something wrong, she's never called me this early in the morning?*

Just looking at her name on my caller I.D. makes me nervous and just like that, sweaty hands are back. Seven in the morning, this can't be good. My mind stops racing to have a real thought., *It could be about my son!*

I answer and immediately run out of the office down the hallway and out the building, just in case this call gets nasty.

I hear her voice. "Hello?"

I answer, "Yeah, I'm here. What's wrong? Is everything okay?"

She says, "Yeah, no, everything is fine."

I mask the last of my concern. "Okay. Well I'm at work, how can I help you?"

She says, "I wanted to call because I felt bad about our last conversation and I thought about it, about you wanting to see your son."

I try not to get too excited. "Yeah?"
"I thought about it and I decided that you do deserve to see him."

My heart jumps. A *huge smile* is on my face right now.
She asks, "Would you like to see him today?"

I immediately respond. "Of course!"
She says, "Okay. What time do you get out of work?"

"I usually stay 'til seven pm, but I can leave at five!" I can't mask my excitement.

She agrees. "Okay, let's plan for you to see him today. Can you do that?"

"Of course!"

"Can you be at the fast food place near our old condo by 5:30 tonight?" It isn't unreasonable, it's a public place, and we both know it.

I agree. "Absolutely!"

"Let's plan to meet there, then. I should get going. I have to get him ready for daycare."

I'm ecstatic. "Okay, and hey!"
She asks, "Yes?"

"Thank you!"

She says, "Just make sure you are there and don't keep us waiting."

We hang up. I throw my hands in the air and do a happy dance as if I just won the gold medal for the 400-yard dash in record time at this year's Olympics! How ecstatic am I right now! Refocus. *Remember you still have a job to do and a promise to keep with your boss.* I should get back inside. After all, my boss doesn't pay me to do happy dances outside in the parking lot.

I make my way back up the stairs and into to the office. I feel amazing! Part of me can't believe that I just got off the phone with my ex and that I'm about to see my son! I haven't seen him since going homeless and since the day of our eviction. Before I make my first phone call for work I text Kent and let him know that I'm leaving today at five p.m. sharp. I even tell him that it's because I'm going to see my lil' man for the first time in months immediately after. He knows this very important to me because we've spoken about it in our car rides. I ask him to be on time. He messages back, "OK."

I must be honest. It's going to be hard to focus today knowing that in just ten hours I'm going to see my son, but I should remember what I'm here for. I should score some moves, make some money and make clients happy. I buckle down; calm myself just enough to make my first call. Never mind that mess I said before about being tired, now I am amped up! I knew today was going to be an amazing day!

I start to hammer out some calls. I'm taking inbound calls, I'm making outbound calls. I'm calling my own mama, "Hey! So, I think you need to move. Like to a different state and like right now! And you need to move with me!" Just kidding, but I would have, if I knew that she was thinking about moving. I'm taking calls today like a machine. No moves booked that I can count on yet, but I know that they are in here somewhere. The morning passes by very quickly. It's almost lunch and I haven't booked any moves yet. It's time for me to reassess and see where I am at for the day. How come I haven't booked any moves yet? Do I need to make changes to my pitch? Do I sound desperate? Oh, wait—I haven't hit my "Maybe" folder yet! I pounce on it pronto.

Nineteen dials and seven rejections later—*Boom!* I hit one! I book a move for a customer who is moving a five-bedroom house with one room dedicated to fine art from Albuquerque, NM to Boston, MA. The move, plus insurance for the artwork, and storage fees, comes to a total of nine thousand dollars! Who's the man?! Oh, it's on now! All I needed was to book my first move of the day and the rest will start dropping like flies! Subtract nine grand from that fifty thousand in extra moves I promised my manager. Why? Because she paid with a credit card and she paid in full! Should I get premature and dare talk about the commission? Well, just in case you were wondering, nine thousand at a ten percent commission is $900! At twelve percent, what my manager promised me, that's $1,080.

Now you see why I fought so hard for that extra two percent, it pays off, eventually. You know what I just noticed? The day is ending shortly, and I haven't booked any more moves after my $9,000 move this morning, but I've built some great possibilities throughout the day and added them to my "Maybe" folder. We'll see if they pan out as well.

Now that I think of it, I can't risk pitching another move when it's so close to 4:30 anyway. My pitch usually takes about forty-five minutes over the phone per call. That's a long time to be speaking to someone about their upcoming move plus, another pitch would put me over five p.m., and I must see my son at 5:30, and I'm not going to risk seeing him for nothing.

I know what you're thinking. "You pitch for forty-five minutes on every phone call? That's a long time!" I know, but that's because I'm very detailed. Other reps' calls take twenty-five minutes, but for me, when it comes to my customers' moves, I try to find out everything I can about it, to show that I genuinely care and to make sure there aren't any mistakes. I ask a ton of questions like, "Are there any vehicles in your move being moved?" Because we move them as well. What are you moving to and from? How far is your house from the closest sidewalk? What about outside in the shed?" I'll even Google their current address and the address they are moving to on Google Maps to make sure we can get trucks in and out of the area without any issues. I can't risk taking a call and shooting past five p.m, so I pack up early. I do some last minute calendaring to help pass the time and look busy at my desk. I shutdown my computer, look at the clock and notice that it's 4.55. I bite my nails for five minutes at my desk as the clock slowly ticks away. Feelings of becoming anxious and nervous at the same time start to build up inside me. I can't believe in just a half hour I will be seeing my boy again!

I can't even tell you how much I miss my lil' man. I start to daydream about the last time I saw him and being in the delivery room the day he was born. Just as I'm about to become completely lost in my thoughts I look up. It's five! I clock out and I'm out the building before anyone can say, "Bye!" I reach the glass doors to exit the building and get outside, excited not only because it's five p.m., but because I'm officially on my way to see lil' guy. Past the glass doors and down the stairs, I look for Kent's work truck. I scan the parking lot. I look left, I look right. No Kent. "You've got to be kidding me."

I look down at my watch and see that it's 5:05 p.m. I told him this morning that I must see my son today at 5:30 and I told him to be here at 5 p.m. sharp! I look to see if there were any text messages from him that I might have missed, mentioning that he might be late. Nothing. I text him again. "Kent, where are you? It's 5:05?" I hit send and wait for him to respond back. Seconds slip by like minutes. No response. I text again and once again he doesn't respond. I receive nothing from the infamous Kent. It's now 5:12 p.m. That's it, I'm calling his ass. I dial his number and what is this? Wait—*What? You've got to be kidding me, his phone is off? Why is his phone off?* I don't mess with sending him anymore text messages this time, I call Miss Puerto Rico.

Thank god, Miss Puerto Rico answers. "Hello!" I blurt, "Hey! Do you know where Kent is at? I told him this morning that I needed him to pick me up at five p.m. sharp. You won't believe this, but my ex called and we set up a meeting for me to see my son tonight after work. It's way past five and he's not here, not answering his text messages or his phone."

She asks, "Wow! Good for you. Wait, his phone off?"

I say, "It is and it's—"I look down at my watch. "And it's approaching 5:25 right now. I'm going to be late to see him."

Miss Puerto Rico replies, "I don't know. He left home like two hours ago?

Do you want me to text or call him?"

I'm getting frantic. "Both! Yes! Please!"

We hang up. My mind starts to race. *Maybe he got into an accident? Or maybe worse, he's doing this just to be shitty and start some drama. Something he can talk about with his work buddies tomorrow. Where is this asshole?*

Well, it's official, I'm going to be late and it's time to call my ex to let her know. I can't believe it's come to this. The first time I get to see my lil' man since the eviction and going homeless and I should call to tell her that I'm going to be late. This won't look good and this call won't go well. As I dial her number I just know that this is about to suck. She answers and sounds irritated, like she knew that this call was going to happen before it did.

"Hello?"
I stammer quickly, "Hey I'm going to be late. My ride share hasn't picked me up from work yet. I'm actually still at work."

He voice is full of contempt. "No surprise, you disappoint once again."

I begin, "No, I'm serious. It's not my..." I stop before I could get to "fault." She's heard it all before. She wouldn't believe it wasn't my fault anyways. I correct myself, hoping to be able to keep this appointment with her to see my lil' man. I swallow my pride and say, "You're right. I'm sorry, but I will be there as soon as possible."

There's only silence on her end.

I ask, "Hello?"
She finally says, "We just pulled up. We're here."

I am almost begging when I say, "Just wait there for me. I'll be there. I promise!" Full irritation has set in at this point on both her and my ends because of Kent. She signs. "Yep."

She immediately hangs up on me.

I drop my head in shame. I hate proving her right. It's now 5:35 and Kent is thirty-five minutes late. He's officially ruined my opportunity to make a positive first impression with my ex and my son. I'm 100% pissed the fuck off and completely infuriated.

CHAPTER SIXTEEN
A reminder

CHAPTER SIXTEEN
A reminder

IT'S 5:40 P.M. AND KENT IS NOW FORTY MINUTES LATE TO PICK ME UP from work and I am officially ten minutes late to see my lil' man. I told him that I needed him to pick me up at work at five o'clock sharp. I had an appointment with my ex to see my son for the first time since the day we were evicted. This mental image keeps repeating in my head of Kent finally pulling up, of me getting in his work van, and before he can say two words, I punch him straight in the mouth. Don't get me wrong, I'm not a violent person, but this is an incredibly important moment in my life and he knows how important this meeting was for me.

"I can't believe he…" Before I can finish that thought I hear what might be his work van coming into the parking lot from the back entrance behind my building. It better be him, it's about six p.m. and there aren't any other cars in the parking lot. Everyone has now gone home, and there's absolutely no reason for anyone to be pulling into the lot this late at night. I'm figuratively biting my nails as I eagerly look in the direction of where the noise is coming from. *This better be him,* keeps running through my head as I notice that the headlights of the vehicle approaching becoming brighter. The vehicle turns the corner. I breathe a sigh of relief. It is him. He better not say one word to me the entire way there because I'm still livid. He pulls up and comes to a full stop. I open the door and jump in.

Kent says, "What's up?"
I immediately glare at him.
"Don't what's up me? Really? I mean really?"

He looks away from me with no explanation. "McDonald's, right? Which one?"

"Lake Mead and Buffalo. Pronto." "You got to be fuck'n kidding me."

And of course, I get no apology from him. I text my ex to let her now I'm now on the way. He puts the van in drive and attempts what can only be called a 'Half assed attempt' at an apology which doesn't feel authentic at all. He goes into his excuse why he was late not knowing that I spoke to Miss Puerto Rico and she told me that he left her house two hours ago. I'm not listening and completely shut him out at this point. He doesn't deserve my ear at this point. Shutting people out to stay focused is a skill I picked up from my old soccer coach in school. My coach back in the day had a rule and his rules could never be broken. The most important rule was the one he applied on the bus, going and coming back to and from away games.

What was this rule? His rule was that no one could talk *at all* during the entire bus ride to and from the game, not even a whisper. If you were ever caught speaking or whispering, you could expect to sit out the first twenty minutes of the game and to do sprints up and down the field beforehand. And definitely didn't want that. It didn't matter if the away game was 15 minutes away or 15 hours away, no speaking on the bus, period. I'm envisioning that bus ride right now in Kent's work truck.

Before every bus ride my coach would say, "You know the rules. No speaking. Not even a whisper." I like to think that he was, in his own way, trying to tell us to use this time to focus on the game, to visualize, to see ourselves on the field, playing our positions, and breaking up plays. I always pictured him saying instead, "Use this time to picture yourself scoring goals. See yourself having your perfect game and just realize that you will be playing as a team with nothing but one goal in common: To play your best!" That's what I always imagined him saying, but the words he spoke are the ones that stuck with me forever. So, on this drive that's exactly what I am doing, not saying a whisper and focusing on the win, getting to my son.

I'm envisioning walking into McDonald's and making my way to the playground area. I see my lil' man and my lil' man sees me, he starts to run in my direction with his arms wide open, looking to get his arms around my legs and hug me. I pick him up and look over at my ex, she's sitting down at a table. She looks happy and my son's smiling, so I know he's happy, which makes me happy. I'm not dumb enough to believe that we will ever be one big happy family again. I know that will never happen, but my vision is instead, "We're all healthy, doing well and together for the moment and that's why we're happy."

My concentration is then broken. Kent can't seem to shut the fuck up. He also can't stop speaking about and rambling on and on about himself. He gets my attention by telling me that he is going to be leaving me at McDonald's. That he's not staying or waiting and that he's had a long day. No surprise there. His attitude is, 'If there is nothing in it for Kent, then why wait?'

"Yeah, whatever dude" is my response.

Luckily, from my job to the McDonald's is just a quick ten-minute car ride, because I don't know how much longer I can stay in the car and listen to this guy. We somehow make it to McDonald's in eight minutes.

As we pull into the parking lot, I immediately see my ex's car. It's a white four door Mitsubishi sedan. The same exact car with Idaho plates that I saw her drive off in the day we got evicted from our condo. Her car alone brings me back to that day instantaneously. Kent brings the van to a complete stop and I hop out. I also turn around before closing the door to grab my bag. I make sure to tell him to be on time tomorrow morning, and that I'm not happy about this evening.

He says, "I know and then blah, blah, blah."

I can't tell you what his response really was. I could care less plus; my mind was racing so fast knowing who and what is waiting for me inside. I close the door and Kent takes off. I'm staring at the main entrance from the middle of the parking lot, scared stiff as the "What ifs" start to take over my thoughts again. What if he doesn't remember me? What if he doesn't love me anymore?

What if my ex and I get into it right in the middle of the McDonald's? What if...

A horn blares.

I'm snapped back into reality. This time it's because of some guy behind the wheel of a white Cadillac. I hear, "Are you crazy? Get out of the middle of the parking lot! I'm trying to get dinner over here!" My bad, who would have thought that day dreaming in the middle of a McDonald's parking lot would be so dangerous? I raise my left hand as if to say, "I apologize," and make my way towards the entrance. I walk in the front door and head over the playground area. My muscles start to tighten up. My senses start to heighten. It's becoming harder to breathe at this moment and just as I turn the corner, I see my ex. She's in jeans and wearing a white blouse. She apparently came here straight from work, it must have been a casual day in her office today.

She doesn't see me, though. Her back is to me and she's looking out towards the play area, specifically by the slide. Knowing that she is looking in that direction because lil' man must be somewhere around there, I immediately look there as well. I don't see him yet. I make my way up to her and eventually end up standing to her left. She was never good at being observant of her surroundings.

I was hoping that she would notice me first so that I would not have to be the one that breaks the ice. As if this wasn't nerve racking enough because she hasn't noticed that I'm standing here, I now must be the one to say something. I eventually get up the courage to say something.

"Hey!" She lets out a loud scream. "Oh my gosh! I didn't know you were standing there. You scared me." She starts to finish her sentence when my attention immediately moves towards the playground. I see...him. My gosh, he's so big. He comes out from the slide area. Hearing his mom scream must have been all he needed to come running.

Time has slowed as my heart drops. I'm in awe with how big he's gotten.

"He's so big!" I say in amazement.

"He is. He's getting taller every day!" My ex says. He runs up to her and stands in front of her motioning for her to give him something to drink. The last time I saw him he was no taller than from the ground up to my knee. Now, he's half way passed my upper thigh.

What? He knows how to ask for something to drink? When did this happen? are thoughts that run through my head. I also start to think, *what else have I missed?*

She drops her hand down and gives him something to drink out of a kid's cup with a lid and a straw on it. Powerade, I'm assuming. It better not be soda! Here I go, I've been here for a mere twenty seconds and I'm already trying to run things. *Wait a minute, he's drinking out of straws now? When did this happen?* I'm starting to get the impression of how much I've missed. I drop my bag and go down to my knees so that I can see him eye to eye.

"Oh my god, my lil' man. Remember me? I'm your dad…" My words start to get away from me. I can't finish without tearing up. I take him in my arms and begin to pick him up. Wow! He's so big. He's amazing. I look him over like the first time I saw him in the delivery room. Both feet, check! All his fingers, hands, ears, eyes, head, check! I bring him in closer to my chest and hug him. I don't want to let him go, ever again. He starts kicking. My daddy instincts kick in and I know that he wants to get down, but not without Daddy getting one more second of hugging him. Smothering him from excessive hugging is something that I don't want to do so I let him down.

As soon as his feet hit the ground he's off and running back to the playground. Man, he's fast. I watch him run back to the slide. My ex and I use this time to start some small talk. We'll call her Mary.

Mary says, "Well, you look good! You look really skinny. You've lost a lot of weight. Have you been eating?"

I shrug a little. "Yes. I have been. I have been on a new weight loss strategy."

She asks, "What is it?"

I try to hint to her about my situation. "Eating cookies out of garbage cans." She politely laughs, not knowing it's the truth.

I'm immediately confused after her comment about me looking good. Tons of emotions and thoughts start whirling around inside me. I'm not sure if she was just being polite with her comment. Is she concerned about me or flirting with me? Is she saying that after all that I've done and after all this time apart that I might still have a chance? I don't know. I can't think about that now though, I'm here to see my son and right now, I want to go play with him. I excuse myself and make my way over to the playground. I find him trying to spark up a conversation with a young girl about four years old over by the ball pit. I tell him with a smile, "You know she's too old for you right." It's so funny to see him trying to chat it up with a girl. Chip off the old block, what can I say? The last time I saw him he was just getting his feet under him, learning to walk. Now he's trying to have conversation with a four year old girl, incredible. He can't speak yet, being just fourteen months old, but he's motioning and pointing at the slide and at the bouncing room inside the playpen. Making sounds as if to say, "See, this is a slide and see, this is a bouncy room."

He's literally showing her around as though it was his house and he's on one of those shows where celebrities show off their houses! Seriously. It's absolutely and incredibly cute. I continue to follow him everywhere. Every time his little feet take a misstep, or if he looks as if he might fall, I'm picking him up right before he has a chance to hit the ground. Even after I catch him I'm asking him, "Are you okay? Are you hurt?" I'm such a wussy dad right now. We play. I take him to the bathroom and change his diaper. It's funny. Daddy instincts kick in immediately as soon as I saw him as if I never missed a day.

It's almost as if I had been here the entire time. I smell something even remotely different and it's, "Oh! It's poopy time," with diaper bag in tow, and off to the bathroom we go. The smell of baby poop, once you open that diaper, is the one thing that you can never get used to, no matter how much time has passed since the last time you've changed a diaper. Once he's changed, I grab the diaper bag and we head back to the playground for some more play time, and then back to the bouncy room. This time I have a little fun and I get in with him. The other parents have no idea what's going on and stare at me either like I'm crazy, or, I hope, the best Dad in the world. They are probably staring because I don't think Dads are allowed in the bouncy pen. There must be weight restrictions or a limit, at the minimum, an age limit! We play for another forty minutes or so and I become incredibly pooped. I feel like I've run a marathon. It's probably a mix of not eating and exerting a lot of energy at the same time trying to keep up with him.

No matter what, it's been awhile since we've done this, and daddy is need of a time out. I make my way back to the table where Mary is sitting. She can tell I'm pooped, no pun intended.
Mary asks, "Tired already?"
I admit it. "Heck yeah."
Mary says, "He is a ball energy."
I nod and catch my breath. "You said it!"

To be honest, I must admire the fact that she is there, in the vicinity but keeping her distance as well. This is cool of her. She's giving me the respect to enjoy this time that I have with him right now, which is surprisingly cool of her.

I make my way back to her table where the diaper bag and stroller is sitting. She has no idea that I went homeless the day of the eviction. I wonder how she would respond or if she would even care if I told her. I don't even know if I'm in the right mind to talk about it even if I did tell her. The experience still haunts me today, and even though I have a roof over my head, I'm still homeless mentally. I don't have any money yet, I'm still eating left-out bread and eating stale cookies from my roommate's garbage just to be able to put something in my stomach. She has no idea that I have been literally eating once a day and ingesting no more than 300 calories a day. For some reason, I want to tell her. I don't know if it's because I'm looking for sympathy or if it's because I want her to feel bad about not taking me with her when they left me to fend for myself. I somehow get the nerve to try and tell her.

I begin with, "Remember when you said I looked skinny?"

Mary watches my son out of the corner of her eye, "Yeah."

I say, "Well, that's what happens when you're only eating once a day"

She nods.

A poor attempt at trying to tell her that I went homeless the day of our eviction, I know, but obviously, she's somewhere else right now or that comment went right over her head. Which one? I don't know. Anyhow, the subject changes and we chat a little bit.

Mary asks, "What have you been doing? What have you been up to?"

I tell her, "Nothing much. I found a job. I'm only making eight bucks an hour, but I'm looking to go on commission soon which will be more money, hopefully."
She says, "That's good."
"Are you still working at the firm?" I prod.

She nods. "Yes."
"Still a paralegal?"
"Yes."
"That's good." We watch my lil' man play. I try not to expect much from this conversation.

She finally says, "It's safe to say that they don't like you anymore and that the same goes for me." She's talking about her boss and the other paralegals at her work. I knew them because of her, and up to this point, had a good relationship with them.

I give a little shrug and say, "That's understandable."

Besides that, poke, our conversation is cordial. For now, we can forget about telling her about me going homeless, even though I still want to share my experience with her. From sleeping on Eric's floor in his office to picking up change from off the ground to collect enough to get something to eat, from room shopping with rolled nickels to my living on only five dollars a day. All of it, but for now, it can wait.

Just then my son comes makes a dash over to our table with a smile on his face as wide as Texas. To my surprise, he makes his way directly to me! He motions for me to pick him up. This kid just melts my heart. I pick him up and place him on my knee. He's a lot heavier than I remember. He points at the small Ice Cream in a cup that Mary has been put to the side. "Oh really, that's why you got on my knee!" Dang, he's smart. The ice cream cup is slightly melted and seems to have been set aside as a treat for him for later. I ask Mary, "Is this yours or his?"

She says, "His."
I point at the cup. "Can I give him some?"
"Sure."
I grab the ice cream in the cup and a spoon and begin to feed him. He eats the entire thing in practically under forty seconds! He almost eats my hand with it!

I joke, a little sarcastic, "My gosh, are you even feeding him?"
She snorts, "Yeah, and he can eat, too! He has *your* appetite.

He starts to start squirming on my lap and is beginning to get cranky. I look down at my phone. Wow, it's 8:30 pm and we've been here for a total of two, if not more, hours. Back in the day in our old condo, it would be bath time and then bed for this little rascal, and if she has him on the same schedule, which I'm sure she still does, I know wherever they are living that he'd be sleeping right now. She always loved being scheduled.

I suggest, "You guys should get going. He's getting cranky."
Mary says, "Yeah, by now, normally, he'd be getting ready for bed."

Damn I'm good.

So, that's exactly what we do. We pack up his diaper bag, his stroller and make our way out of McDonald's. I carry him, I choose not to put him in the stroller. I want to enjoy this moment of being able to carry him out to the car. Also, knowing that our meet today is ending, I can't put him down yet. We make it outside to where I saw her car when I first got here, and I open the back-passenger door and strap him into his car seat. I kiss him like thirty-nine times on the forehead, but not before looking at him long enough to where I can remember his image and hold it in my head forever.

I eventually close the door and turn to Mary.
"It's late, you should get him home."

Mary nods. "I agree. When do you want to see him again?"

My immediate thought is, *I'm sorry, but is it my birthday? You mean I get to see him again?* There's a party going on in my head right now as we make plans for me to see him. Two weeks from today. I'm ecstatic! She lifts her hand up for a handshake.

We shake hands, she walks around to the front of the car and gets in to leave. No hugs today, but someday soon. Even if we never rekindle what we once had, I am blessed to have someone in his life that takes care of him the way that she does so well. He is a happy boy and it's because of her. No matter what our differences are, no one can ever take away from her the fact that she's a great mother.

She eventually starts the car, backs up and takes off. I watch them as they go. As I'm standing in the middle of the parking lot once again, and as if he could see me out of the back window, I slowly wave goodbye and watch them leave. I turn around knowing that my night isn't over yet. I don't have a car and there is no rideshare waiting for me tonight. With just lint in my pocket and no money for a taxi, it looks like I'm walking. I take my phone out of my pocket and open the web browser.

I Google the address of the McDonald's that I'm at and then my address. Let's see how far I am from home from this McDonald's. Twelve miles, geesh, but after seeing my lil' guy today for the first time in months, this walk home is going to be totally worth it.

I take a left and start to walk. I start to recall that famous quote and it couldn't be any more relevant than it is right now. "The journey of a thousand miles begins with a single step." This couldn't be any more relevant or ironic than it is right now, because I'm doing and have done exactly that tonight.

CHAPTER SEVENTEEN

Nothing comes easy

CHAPTER SEVENTEEN

Nothing comes easy

IT'S FIVE IN THE MORNING and I'm just getting back from my walk. It took me about an hour to walk out and walk back home. I woke up at three-thirty this morning and for the most part, I've been getting better at getting up in the mornings and sticking to the decision I made to start taking walks. Even though I have my headphones on and I have my thoughts, I starting to find myself becoming bored with my walks in the morning. I'm thinking of stepping up my game and possibly getting a bike. Maybe something that is meant for the street like a road bike. I could find a cheap, older one online if I put some energy into it. If it's in great shape, who really cares how old it is?

I take a long shower. I'll never get over the satisfaction of being able to take a shower. It's amazing, the simple things that you miss when you go without. I get dressed. I make my way to the kitchen and grab a package of ramen and make a quick peanut butter sandwich for breakfast. I can't afford jelly right now. Don't feel bad for me, it's a blessing to have bread and peanut butter that I made with my own two hands in my own kitchen for breakfast, trust me. I look down at my phone, almost quarter to six, I must get going before I'm late for work. I exit the kitchen, turn off all the lights, I make my way out the front door and down to the parking lot to wait for Kent.

Tick tock, tick tock. What a surprise, Kent is not here and officially late, again, for the second day in a row.

This guy has impeccable timing for fucking me over at the most inopportune moments. Today is my first Saturday that I'm working for commissions only. I'm not being paid to come into the office today, so the first ones in the office and on the phones, will be the first ones to walk away with commissions in their pockets. Timing is important and right now I don't have the time to deal with Kent's shit. Speaking of work, I've been killing it! I've been on fire and from my calculations, I've closed enough moves to get close to that fifty-grand mark I set for myself in sales this month. What's exciting is the fact that I'll be making my first commissions check ever!

Once I hit the fifty thousand dollars in moves this month my boss has agreed to give me a twelve percent commission on all my sales. If you are doing the math, I know I am, I'm looking at a maximum of six thousand in potential commissions coming to me in my next paycheck. This is the first time in several months after going homeless that I have had a chance to make *real* money! This check is going to change everything.

I can already imagine what I will do with the money. I'm going to get my lil' guy some new clothes, enough food for the month, pay for his daycare for the month and get him some diapers to go along with it. For myself, I'm going to get a road bike to replace my walks in the morning, *fill up my refrigerator with real food,* buy some practical second-hand clothes, and get a pair of real sneakers. I'm so tired of taking walks in the morning in work shoes. I'll get a used bed, so I can finally stop sleeping on the floor in my bedroom, maybe a dresser and dare I say it...possibly a car?

The possibilities of what I'm going to do with my six thousand dollars are endless! More like $4,500 after taxes, but it's all good. Just as my daydreaming reaches an all-time high, Kent casually rolls up, as if he doesn't owe me to be here on time or something. Just as he starts to roll up and come to a stop to let me in, something in my gut tells me that, this might be the last time I see Kent, ever. I don't know why or for what reason, but I just know. I can feel it.

He pulls up and comes to a complete stop. I get in and it's the same ol' routine when I get in his work truck. No apologies for being late and the same old blah, blah, blah. How he's a God-given gift to Miss Puerto Rico because he's a single guy willing to date a single mother with kids. How her kids are devil spawn and how he shouldn't have to discipline kids that aren't even his, because she supposedly doesn't. As a friend, I really like Miss Puerto Rico and it's hard having to hear this guy talk shit about someone I like. It's difficult because this guy is my ride to and from work, even though he's always late and a complete asshole.

His conversations about himself and being a gift in Miss Puerto Rico's life is eventually cut short, thanks to a quick right and entering the parking lot to my job. He drops me off and I head upstairs to the office, extremely excited to get my day started and to end, because at 4:30 they'll be handing out the commission checks.

Do I really have to go through this entire day? *Isn't there a fast forward button somewhere around here that I can press to hurry this day up and get me to 4:30 pm?* I say to myself. A smile comes to my face and I make my way up the stairs to our office.

Finally, I make it to the office and to my desk. I put my stuff away, log on, plug in and go. Dialing away like a machine. I can't help but want to work hard; I have a deep appreciation for my new job.

Maybe it's because the harder I work, the more I see myself getting away from my experience of being homeless, or maybe it's the fact that this place was the only place that gave me and my—at the time of my interview—full grown ratty beard, unkempt hair, smelly (from sleeping on the streets), ripped clothing a shot, when everyone else said no. Or maybe it's because I really like the moving industry and that I really like helping people. What I do know is this: I really like the feeling and knowing that I am making a difference in people's lives. Even if it's just helping them with their long distance move.

I mean, think about it, you're moving from one side of the country to the other. An example would be Miami, FL to California. You're leaving what's comfortable: your friends, family, co-workers, your support system, your dentist, family doctor, the list goes on. You must pick up everything, only to be dropped off somewhere on the other side of the country where you know no one and have to rebuild all by yourself. Without the comforts of your friends, family and your support system. You move your entire life and your house.

You move your kids and a pet. On top of your move you have to deal with booking rooms, airfare and only getting a set amount of time off work to make it happen. It's scary and, not to mention, stressful.

That's where I come in. I (at my best) try to alleviate some of that stress with your move by reassuring you that I am here to help and that I care. I personally moved from New Jersey to Las Vegas by myself and I know firsthand how much the stress of a cross country move can have on you. So, by hiring only credible moving companies and only professional movers with impressive FMCSA (Federal Motor Carrier Safety Administration) records, and by making sure that the moving company that moves you understands you. The reason for your move, is how I show how I care. I do this by being as detailed as possible with you over the phone so that I can pass on those same details to our movers so that they can get an impression of how important this move is, outside of booking the move itself. Maybe this is why I'm booking so many moves lately, or it could be as simple as I'm just grateful for what I'm doing and the opportunity that I have to do it.

I'm twenty-four minutes into a pitch and I can feel the vibration of my phone in my pocket alert me. My phone starts to go off like crazy. All text messages, three in a row. What the heck? I reach down in my pocket in the middle of my pitch to grab my phone and to see what the heck is going on.

Who the heck is texting me like a madman? It's Kent.

His text message reads:
"Miss Puerto Rico wants to know who much you will be giving her today."

I quickly text back," $350."

Kent hits back with, “Plus the extra $50?”

I reply, “Yes, only if she shows up so that I can give it to her personally myself.”
Kent gives no response after that.

I stand strong. I’m not about to allow him to run me for an extra fifty bucks a week, especially when I know Miss Puerto Rico isn’t asking for it. She would have sent me a text if it was

really for her. I would have heard something. I know he just wants to pocket the extra fifty a week for free lunches on me, and I’m not having it. If it is really for Miss Puerto Rico then I’ll give it to her directly because she has kids and the extra fifty a week will help her. I know it will go to a good place and not to someone else’s back pocket. His silence only indicates that he didn’t like my last text. I get back on the phones and three pitches later it’s about noon. My boss finally makes his way into the office for the first time today. It’s been a slow-moving morning, so I guess I’ll warm up my Ramen Noodles and take lunch. I noticed that when my boss walked in that he had envelopes in his hand. That could only mean one thing. Checks, baby! I’ve also noticed that he hasn’t said hi to me or looked in my direction. This entire month, every day except for today, he’s always said hi to me when he came in.

Why wouldn’t he? I’ve been his star pupil since we’ve made our agreement that I would bring him an extra fifty thousand dollars in moves in one month.

I believe I’ve delivered, or at least have come close to it. If he’s in a bad mood, he better snap out of it! Besides, it’s Saturday! Commission day Saturday! Today should be a day of celebration! Anyhow, I eat my Ramen Noodles for lunch and head back to my desk. Before I know it, the day flies by fast! I’ve put in a good four pitches and added them all to my pipeline and to my ‘Maybe’ folder for possible future booked moves. Oh boy! Come on, 4:30 p.m.! I watch as the clock ticks away. Soon it becomes 4:15—4:20—4:25—Come on!

Finally! My boss makes the announcement, “Four thirty. Last call. Hang up your phone’s, sit at your desks and come get your commission check when your name is called out.”

You don't have to tell me twice! I hang up my phone and my computer is shut down in less than three seconds. He starts to call out names. Top producers are obviously being called first. It's obvious because the guys that he is calling up first are known for putting up big numbers. Even so, this shouldn't take long since there are only seven employees here. He calls one employee after the other. I'm starting to get restless in my chair. What the heck? When are you going to call my name? Just before I can finish that thought, he calls me. That's me! No other names are called after me. I guess not everyone made commissions this week? I walk up to his desk and grab my first commission check like it's my freaking diploma, like I've won something.

I say thanks and run back to my desk. Open it or don't open it? I should open it; I'm too excited to wait until I get home to see those zeros. I feel it's Christmas day and not only did I just pick up the last present under the tree, but this present just so happens to have my name on it! I rip the side of the envelope my check came in as to not damage the check when I open it. My hands are sweaty. Why do they make these things so hard to open? I grab the check by the corner and pull it out of the envelope. I look left to make sure my name is on it, it is. Of course, my eyes automatically scroll to the right to check the amount and...Um, $398.16? What the fuck?

What the flying fuck?

I flip my check over to see if there's another check on the back. Nope, nothing. I flip my check over again back to the front praying that the amount has somehow magically changed. Nope, nothing. I can't believe this.

$398.16? You've got to be kidding me! Is this a joke? I'm in shock. I was expecting a minimum of a $4,500 commission check. I know I didn't sell my promised $50,000 in moves yet, but I still can. I easily closed $45,000 in additional moves since my boss and I made our agreement and at $45,000 in moves at ten percent commission, I should have a check in my hand in the amount of $4,500 before taxes. This isn't a joke, this is very real, and my eyes at not playing tricks on me. I just got fucked.

I look over at my boss. He's looking down at his desk. His head hangs low. He knows. He knew.

That's why he didn't say anything to me all day. That's why he gave me my check last. He set me up. He knew I would be pissed and he gave my check last hoping I wouldn't open it or cause a scene. I need to calm down because my blood is about to boil over. I calmly get up and make my way over to his desk. I stand over his left shoulder and I say,

"We need to talk, outside. Now!"

My boss mumbles, "Yep."

He had to have known that this was coming. He gets up and makes his way slowly toward the front door, almost like a child that has been caught telling a lie and now knows that they're about to meet their fate. We get outside the office door. As soon as it closes shut behind us, all bets are off. He's not my boss at this point, he's a thief and he just stole everything that I have been dreaming of doing with my commission check in a matter of minutes.

The one thing you should know about me is that I do not play when it comes to money, especially if it's money that I had to work very hard for. I worked hard. I worked with laser like focus, without any distractions, I leveraged every second I was behind my desk to make sure I did everything I could to make him and his office a lot of money. We had a deal and he reneged, but at this point, believe it or not, he's going to pay up one way or another.

I growl, "What the fuck is this?" I wave my pathetic excuse for a commission paycheck in front of his face.

He looks at it and with a tone of audacity says, "It's a check!"
"Oh? You're an asshole now? You know what I mean. What the fuck is this?"

He starts to babble which only sounds like a poor attempt to recite a speech he had planned in his head for this exact moment. I have no idea what he's saying. My frustration only grows deeper, so I cut him off.

"Where's my $4,500 dollars?"

He says, "Remember in our initial interview? I told you that we would pay you a base salary up to the point where you started to commission out regularly and then, at that point, when you get paid, you would have to pay back every paycheck that we gave you in the interim."

I'm shocked. "Wait? What? What are you talking about man? You never said that!"

He says, "Yes, I did. And not only will you pay back every paycheck we've ever written you but, you will also have to pay back for your seat, your phone, your computer, and pay ten percent to help with the rent."

It's taking everything I have right now not to choke him out, for principle and stupidity alone.

I almost begin to scream. "Are you mental? You never told me that when you hired me, because if you would have, I would have told you that you could shove this job straight up your ass!"

He folds his arms. "I don't appreciate your tone of voice right now."

I retort, "Well I don't appreciate people stealing from me; in the streets or by a boss."

I shout, "And I guess that's what you do, huh? Fuck people out of their money? Is that why there are only seven employees here? Is that why there isn't anyone who's been working here for ninety days or more? Because it takes them that long to commission out and when they finally do, they finally find out that they're being fucked by their boss!"

He says, "I guess you've just given your resignation?"

At this point, I have a moment of clarity. I start to notice just how cool my manager is acting and how he hasn't tried to defend himself or justify what he's done at all, under the circumstances. I start to realize he's done this before, many times before, and that I'm right about the ninety-day thing. I also just now realize that I will never see that money, ever. They've been doing this for a long time and he pretty much have this down to a science.

I declare, "You don't have to guess if this is my resignation because it is, I quit! This isn't going to be the last time you hear from me, either! I'm going straight to the labor board!"

He shrugs. "Go ahead and good luck!"
His answer is kind of puzzling. I'm taken aback for a moment.

He says easily, "Been there, done that and you're not threatening me. By the time you head down to the labor board and they find out who we are and file their case, we have already closed shop, changed our office, and changed our company name and phone. You, on the other hand, would have wasted your time. So, go right down to the labor board. Have fun with that."

I grunt, "Done this before?"
He smiles, and his smile could not look any more evil than it looks right now. He says, "More times than you can imagine."

And like that I'm done. I leave him in the hall and head back inside to clean out my desk. It's important that I to try not to make a show of it and stay professional. I never say anything to disrupt the sales floor. I have too much respect for myself and my co-workers to do that. I never raise my voice or give any indication that anything is wrong, but then again, I don't have to. I grab my phone, bag, check, notes, and a printout of my sales since I've been there. This will provide excellent proof for the labor board. Even though I know I'll never see that money, I want to have proof that I've created a personal sales goal and came close to achieved it. I leave the office without saying goodbye to anyone. I'm halfway down the hallway in my building when I text Kent. "Can you come pick me up? I just quit." I make it outside the glass doors where I once sat freezing on my first day of work and head away from the building. I walk down the stairs out past the parking lot and find myself continuing to walk. I can't stop walking, I'm so infuriated. I make a couple of laps around the parking lot before I realize that Kent has yet to text me back. I sit down on the corner, take out my phone and send him another text. "Dude, I just quit. Where are you at?"
Finally, he replies, "I can't be there for another hour and 45 minutes" He never ceases to amaze me. I put my phone in my pocket. I'm completely frustrated. I can't help but feel like I can't get a break. As soon as I get something going that's positive, something else steps in and destroys me. I can't help but

think that I either did something incredibly brave, or something incredibly stupid by quitting my job. I let my emotions get to me, yeah, I got that, but if I was to stay there and continue to work for him, I would have given him the impression that it's ok to shorten my paycheck at any time he plans. That I don't stand for anything and I'll fall for anything. Not to mention, I work on commission only! If I don't work I don't get paid, it's literally that simple. It's not like he's paying me to just show up or hang out there. To continue to work there knowing that he will shorten my commission check again would just piss me off even more. So, yeah, I just quit my one and only job and again, I don't have an income, but I let him know that he will not be able to use me. How do you put a price tag on that?

And I just remembered, I must give Miss Puerto Rico her share of my final paycheck, $350. After I subtract her $350, I'll be left with $48.17. Hopefully she'll work with me and understand that I'm not going to be seeing any more paychecks until I get a new job.

The good news is that at this point, I've paid everyone off. I've paid my roommate; I've paid Miss Puerto Rico and if we work something out, hopefully, I will have enough money to buy a cheap road bike for transportation after. From this point on I will have to be even pickier about where I work and be certain to read the fine print. To make sure they fucking pay. I'm currently out $4,601.83 and I can officially say goodbye to that new car I wanted, taking care of my son, filling up my fridge with food, but the good news is, thanks to Kurt not being able to pick me up right away, I have an hour and forty-five minutes to formulate a plan and figure things out.

This isn't a negative, it's a positive. As for them, they'll get theirs one day. The universe has a way of doing that, getting even with people for me.

As for me, there's a message here, I can feel it. I just should find out where the message is and use it for power moving forward. For whatever I do next. It's really that simple. In the meantime, fuck these guys.

CHAPTER EIGHTEEN
I quit

CHAPTER EIGHTEEN
I quit

I'VE OFFICIALLY QUIT MY JOB. I've been sitting on the same corner on the same sidewalk outside my old job since about 4:30. I'm waiting for my ride, Kent, to pick me up. It's about six o'clock now, and as I hurry up and wait, I have no other choice but to go over in my head what just happened... and it sucks.

I tell you, no one knows how to kick me when I'm down like I do. The conversations in my head are sometimes the worst conversations you can have with anyone. When I was homeless they were intense, negative. I've had thoughts of suicide and even planned a few out as far as how I would do it. What bus I would jump in front of. How fast that bus would have to be traveling to kill me so that I would not end up in the hospital missing limbs, or worse, end up as a vegetable. What's funny is that after I had made the decision to die, I realized that I was too chicken to do it and in that moment, I heard a whisper in the back of my head say 'You are better than this.' I can honestly say that almost immediately, there came an immense feeling of wanting to live that came over me. I was no longer willing to accept eating out of garbage dumpsters. I was no longer willing to spend my life sleeping on the ground or being a smelly beggar that the world wished would just disappear. I started to mentally get back on my feet again. It's almost like that voice pushed me to make my decision to do something about my situation. I immediately changed my thoughts, and they became a lot more positive! I started to think of ways to get out and get back to being a normal human being again. It was grand.

However, right now, I should say I'm feeling the depression start to creep in though. It's been a while, but I can still tell you what he looks like. He's a tall, black shadow that likes to take up space in my head and when he speaks, he says things like, "Man, what did you do? You're so stupid." The emotions are a little too much to take right now. I start to tear up. "You should have thought this out before quitting, you moron. You should have swallowed your tongue, collected a few more paychecks, and then planned your exit like a normal person does."

He likes to speak like that, in terms of *you should've* or *could of.* "Just weeks after being homeless, without an income, here you are again, on the verge of becoming homeless once again. Great job...Loser"

I try to block him out and ask myself some real quality questions, instead of talking in *woulda, coulda, shoulda.* planning questions like, "What am I going to do now? What am I going to eat next week?"

I start to take inventory of what I have back at home in my head. I'm almost out of food. I'm almost out of water. I promised my ex diapers next week, and just like that the thought leaves my mind. This by far is the only time in my life where I am somewhat excited to see Kent. The bright lights from his work van pull my attention away from my thoughts as he pulls into the parking lot to pick me up.

Kent pulls up right beside where I'm sitting and opens the passenger door for me to get in. He's never opened my door before, he must be excited to hear about my pain today and how I quit. "Mr. Egotistical", "Mr. Takes-Pride-In-Other-People's–Pain" can't wait to hear how it went down and it shows. He doesn't even allow me to get into the car first before the first question arrives. As I'm getting up off the ground he's already asking me a ton of questions and it's not because he cares, it's because he feeds off of situations where other people suffer. It's unavoidable, after all he is my ride, so congratulations Kent, today my pain becomes your entertainment. The good news is that my house is only fifteen minutes from here by car. I hop in, strap on my seat belt, and let the 'I'm suffering' games begin.

Kent asks, with a weird level of excitement in his voice, "So, what happened?" He has a little devilish grin on his face and it makes my skin crawl.

I shrug. "I quit."
Kent asks, "I know, but how? Don't leave out any details." How did I know he was going to say that?

I try to play that it was nothing. "I just walked out. I lost my temper and cursed out the boss."

Kent still has that devilish smile on his face and obviously not satisfied with my answers up to this point. "Why?"
I explain, "I was expecting a $4,500 commission check today for the moves that I booked this month and instead, I got this check for $300 and some odd dollars."

He asks, "Wait? How much were you expecting?"
I sigh, "Forty-five hundred bucks."

Kent shrieks, *"What?"*
It's almost funny how at this moment his smile doesn't seem to want to leave his face.

I nod. "Yes, exactly."

He starts in with rapid-fire questions. "What did you do? Did you turn throw any chairs? Flip over and desks? Punch your boss in the face?"

I stay calm. "No. Nothing like that. To be honest, he's not worth it."

He snorts, “I would have punched somebody in the face! There’s that *woulda, coulda, shoulda* again.

Apparently, just quitting my job isn’t entertainment enough for him. He needs to know if I caused a scene before I left because only that would be worthy gossip after he dropped me off.

I’m still calm when I explain, “I’m not that type of person. I’m not the type to cause a scene. Even though I could have and had every right to, I left like a man. A very pissed off man.”

Kent seems almost disappointed right now and says, “So, you didn’t punch anybody’s lights out, flip over any desks or cause a scene?” The dumb grin finally starts to leave his face.

“No. I didn’t. It might not be today, but they will get theirs soon one day.”

He finally asks a practical question. “So, what are you going to do now?”

“I don’t know.”
Kent asks, “You’re still paying me, right?”

I correct him, “You mean am I still going to pay Miss Puerto Rico, right?”
Kent replies, “Um, yeah. Sure. That too.”

I’m not in the mood for him today. “Just an FYI: I’m not going to pay you anything. I’m going to pay Miss Puerto Rico and I’m going to pay her directly, not you. As far as she goes, she will get every penny I promised her. I would never leave her high and dry. Even if it means leaving myself high and dry. By the way, she hasn’t even mentioned anything about wanting any additional money, let alone, an extra $50 a week for rides? Why do you think that is?”
He’s silent.

I continue. “Your girlfriend is a single mom with five kids. Not paying her is not even an option.”

Kent says, “Okay. So, are you going to pay her today?”

"Yes. I'm a man of my word. Even though you have been the one lately who has been giving me rides to and from work, it is she who I made the agreement with. I just hope she allows me to make payment arrangements because I'm going to need this three-hundred-some-odd dollars until I can find another job."

Kent says, "Don't worry, I'll talk to her."

Fuck. Great. I've said too much.

I tell him, "No, it's okay. I'll talk to her."

Kent replies, "No, I insist. Let me talk to her. You've been through a lot today. She'll listen to me. I'll talk to her for you."

I know what that means. It means that he's going to talk her into not accepting my payment arrangements and convince her to no longer give me rides. In his mind, this is his way of pulling the strings, causing drama, and sitting back to watch as the arguments unfold. That's his M.O. and I also know, that this will be the last time and last ride I will be receiving from Kent ever again. I'm going to miss Miss Puerto Rico, and once again, I will find myself without transportation.

Not much is said after his comment about him talking to Miss Puerto Rico about me needing payment arrangements for rides. I believe he knows that this will be the last time that he sees me, too. We finally reach my place. He pulls to a complete stop and says, "Well, good luck to you." He may as well have said, "Good riddance." I don't say anything.

He drops me off and I make my way through the parking lot and head upstairs. I'm not looking forward to, once again, the tireless and endless bullshit job searching on Craigslist and Monster at all. I unlock my door, walk in, throw my bag down on the couch and grab myself a glass of water out of the kitchen. I sit down on the couch and go over the day again. I'm sitting in front of the TV, but the TV isn't on. I'm just staring at it. I start to think about my son and the really pressing questions like, "How am I going to get to him next week to see him? How am I going to explain this to his mom?" Then I remember there's no need to. "She already thinks I'm a loser. She won't believe me anyway."

The way she speaks and thinks about me today isn't only because I was the reason we were evicted. It wasn't only because I made horrible decisions as a man; it was because I had lied to her one too many times. Eight years ago, when we had just met, I was a DJ with the ego and the very large play list of songs to match all of the broken hearts I had collected. I really rarely had thought twice about the hearts that I had broken and because of that, I had been careless with hers.

What I've noticed now is that, at that time in my life, I was a lost child pretending to be living in a man's body. This is something I that haunts me today. I was careless with my past relationships and some might say, her not believing in me, is somewhat justified.

Since then, coupled with going through everything that I've been through, including homelessness, I've matured. I've given up childish things, breaking hearts and since then, I've sworn off lying and promised myself to never mistreat any relationships ever again. Professionally or romantically. If anything, I'm more appreciative of the relationships that I have today and cherish them all with respect and honor.

My mind wanders back to the events that happened today and back to the questions that I have in my head around quitting my job.

How am I going to help my son's mom with his expenses now? I promised I would. How am I going to get to see him now? What happens if he's hungry and looks up at me for something to eat and we're out somewhere? What would I do then?

Then the more important questions arise.

Would my lil' man be proud of me? Are my actions of today representing those of a good role model for him?

I, for some reason, remember Christmas. It's coming up soon. I don't have any time to sitting around praying to find a new job. I need to find one and need to quickly. In the meantime, it looks like I'll be sleeping on the floor in my bedroom and wearing the same two shirts and pants for a lot longer than I expected. I'll tell you something, what's frustrating is life's starts and stops that I'm experiencing. Why can't I just get one good break that lasts? I need one to last because these "Starts and stops" are starting to take their toll on me. The rationales of today's events weigh down on me. The rash decision I made to quit my job, losing my transportation, losing my income, not having enough food in my cabinets to last the week and now not knowing what I am going to do about a job. I just don't know how much longer I can put up this mental and emotional fight.

I fight to stay positive and to keep moving forward. It's tough. I should just give up. I take a deep breath. I know my spirit would never allow me to do that. I've been through too much to give up now. I think that the day has emotionally drained me and that mentally, I'm just tired. Spiritually, I'm exhausted. Still sitting in front of the TV, my eyes start to become tired and heavy. I feel a nap coming on. My roommate isn't home, so I guess I'll take advantage of being able to sleep on the couch. Anything other than the hard floor in my room sounds heavenly right now. Oh look, pillows! I lie down if just for a second and close my eyes. Without any warning, I immediately fall asleep.

It's about 9:30 at night when I wake up. Man, that nap felt amazing! I wake up feeling refreshed, revitalized and re-energized. I also wake up with a clear understanding that, no matter what the conversations was in my head before I fell asleep, I am ultimately happy. I'm happy because of what I've been through and the changes that I've made. I'm happy with my struggle and know that it will make me one day. I'm also happy because I know that I made the right decision to quit my job. Even though I don't have any money coming in and I don't have much food in my cabinets I just remember that, no matter what, that I took a stand for myself, and I'm still better off than where I was a month ago! I remember the "breaks" that I've had along the way.

Eric, for starters, because if it wasn't for him I wouldn't have had an office to sleep in or a computer to look for jobs on or the security of four walls and a roof to sleep under. I remember the break I had with that barber, who allowed me to use his hair clippers for free to shave the beard off my face before I went on all those interviews. I also remember the break my new roommate gave me by allowing me to move in this beautiful condo without paying one cent in security or rent up front. I remember Miss Puerto Rico who gave me a break and allowed me, a stranger, to set up payment arrangements with her in exchange for rides to and from work. I remember because of that, me not having to walk thirty-two miles a day to work. I also remember making that first call to my ex, and being able to reconnect with my son, and to finally see him. It's amazing but I woke up completely confident that I will make it! Again! I'm grateful!

Believe it or not I'm grateful for my last job, too. Even though they royally screwed me out of my commission check, royally I'm grateful because it was them that gave this ex-homeless guy a place to make money, a place to feel responsible again. Out of the nineteen-some-odd interviews that I went on, they were the only ones that gave me a chance, the only ones that would hire me. They took a chance and hired a smelly, dirty, ripped-clothes-wearing, homeless guy who slept on streets corners, without any experience or talent in the position they were hiring for.

I have food, I have a refrigerator to put it in and because of these breaks I'm back to goal setting again. So yes, I lost my job today and yes, they screwed out of four thousand dollars and yes, I lost my transportation and I might not have a lot of food, but guess what? I learned something new today. I learned that if you're going to be successful, and have goals and hit them, that you cannot allow circumstances and excuses to stop you. In order to succeed you must be the first person in the office and the last one out of it. You cannot become a victim of your own "shadow man" or the negative thoughts in your head. You should understand where these thoughts are coming from, acknowledge them and move on. And no matter what, always remain positive and believe in your dreams! With action, it's the only true way out of any bad situation.

What's amazing is that, if you would have asked me before I moved into this condo while I was counting out change to find seventy-five cents to fill my stomach with a bag of chips, if any of this would be possible, I would have told you you're freaking insane. All it took was one decision, and look at me now. It might look to you like I've taken three steps backwards, but guess what? I haven't.

In the mental toughness game, I've taken five steps forward. In life, I will never go back to being homeless ever again and that by itself gives me the drive and motivation to win! Here's an idea? Why don't we get off this couch, go back into my bedroom, lay on the ground, jump on that old dinosaur of a desktop computer and find us another fucking job? What do you say Holis? All juiced up, I'd say it sounds like a fucking plan!

CHAPTER NINETEEN

It's not over

CHAPTER NINETEEN

It's not over

AFTER MY NAP and picking myself up from off the couch, I'm back in my room on the floor. I still don't have a bed. I'm online and looking for a job. The only thing that is different about today than from months ago is, for one, I've showered and for two, I've shaved. Okay, to be honest, everything is different, and everything has changed for the better. Not to mention, I've also showered more than just one time. Now, if only I could find that one job that is going to get me back on track.

Once again, I'm on the hunt. This is the second time I've found myself looking for a job in months. Here goes another round of interviews and strangers telling me that "I'm not experienced enough for the position that they are hiring for" or that "They'll call me after they interview a few more people" which we all know is bull. The worst are the jobs that want you to come back and interview a second, third, and fourth time. They might as well say, "We would love to have you come down here and waste your time, three or four more times before we say no. Is that okay with you?" That would be a lot easier to swallow. The easiest way for me to find a quick job and to be able to skip the redundancies of the interviewing process is to find a job where multiple interviews with the same employer are pointless, where it's one interview and done. Those jobs are manual labor jobs.

I head over to the "Labor" section on Craigslist for search for manual labor jobs. Yep, heavy lifting. The worst part about it is that I'm completely desperate and broke. Remember, I've been paying my roommate and my rideshare back over the last few weeks, so I haven't saved up any money. Every dime I made I had to give away at least nine of it.

I'm submitting my resume everywhere for anything online that will produce quick cash. It's a good thing that summer has passed. If this was just a few months ago, I would have been breaking my back and sweating my butt off in 125-degree desert heat. I could never imagine doing heavy lifting, landscaping, moving people, shoveling tons of rock, cutting grass or washing windows in that heat. I would have died. Winter is a different story.
That kind of work is exactly what I need right now, so I find a few jobs on Craigslist helping people move. Ironic, considering my last job was working for a moving company. This job that I just found is different though, because at my old job, I didn't do any of the hard back-breaking labor. I worked on the phones in a cool, dry, air-conditioned office with comfy chairs. Tonight, everything changes, I'm about to go out and break my back to help someone move their living room and bed set from one apartment to another. The new apartment is on the other side of town. The good news is that she's a single mother, so at the end of the day I can feel good about helping her move.

Her advertisement is also asking for a guy and a truck. Problem, I obviously do not have a truck. I email her anyway and ask her what is she willing to pay for her move and what kind of truck is needed for the job.

She replies, "A pick-up will work just fine. I don't have a lot of things and the pay is $75."

Hmm, this obviously does not work for me. She is asking for moving help from someone who has a pickup truck that can load her stuff and deliver it from one side of the valley to another. Basically a 30-minute drive there, 30-minute drive back and, I'm assuming, about two hours total to loading and unloading time for seventy-five bucks? An hour drive in an average pickup truck will burn up seventy-five in gas by itself. I give it a bit of thought. Finally, I email her with, "If you throw in an additional $50 for gas then you have yourself a deal." A few minutes later she replies with, "Ok. Here is my address. Can you be here at 8pm?"

I reply with, "Of course." And just like that, we're in business but, I'm only halfway there. Now I need to find a guy with a truck! I place an ad on Craigslist myself looking for moving help, stating that I am looking for a guy with a truck. Talk about being creative, this guy, whoever I hire, will be my ride to and from this moving gig and an extra pair of hands if I need him. I only have four hours before I must show up at her apartment with a truck and a driver. Let's see what happens!

As I stare at my email waiting for an answer to come in from my ad, I have a revelation. I pick up my journal and start to write. You know, they say to build something you must first break it down and take it apart. My old life as I knew it has been demolished. It's been, for the lack of a better word, ripped to shreds, broken down, chewed up and spit out; and for what reason? I don't know.

I just know that I've failed. I've failed everyone, but I can tell you one thing though, whatever is coming my way is going to be amazing! What I am going through, this rebuilding, is going to take me higher than I could have ever gone before and when it gets here, I know for sure, I will be made into something great!

I am incredibly thankful for my journal and the ability to write in it every day. It's helped me through these incredibly tough times. I wasn't kidding when I said that I had contemplated suicide and throwing myself in front of a speeding bus. Because of my journal I never did it. So, to this journal, I thank you, for saving my life…more than just once. Please know that one day, I will pay you back and that one day the words that I write in here will be used for something bigger. One day.

Though, for right now, I need to check my email and see if anyone responded to my ad on Craigslist for a "Guy with a moving truck." This guy has got a job to do.

BOOK BREAK

A poem 'Before & After'

Book break

A poem 'Before & After'

Before

I have looked at so much

Yet nothing have I seen

I have traveled so far

But nowhere have I gone

I have love with all I have

Yet nothing I had to give

I have gained so much

Yet nothing do I have

I have spoken a million words

I have listened to the world

But nothing have I heard

For you friend who has failed yet still stands

Book break

A poem 'Before & After'

After

Shallow waters wash away sins

stepping out unto a new world

I feel his grace upon my heart

light that was once out of reach

Now my shelter against the darkness

Leaving behind a world of hurt

Desperation no longer my native tongue

The light flickers upon my soul and grants me everlasting love

Forgiveness promised upon the receipt of my heart

My burdens removed by his words

My former self washed away

in shallow waters.

CHAPTER TWENTY
The introduction of Tanya

CHAPTER TWENTY
The introduction of Tanya

IT'S BEEN AN HOUR and I have received zero phone calls or emails regarding my ad on Craigslist for a driver and truck to help me tonight. I must come up with something quick or I am not going to be able to make this move and a quick fifty bucks for food. The extra fifty I asked her for gas to do the move is going to go to me and the seventy-five she offered originally is going to whoever helps me with this move. After all it's their truck that's going to help me make this possible.

So, I changed some of the wording and re-posted the ad with the changes. I also set up a few new spam emails just for re-posting this ad a few more times under the labor section. Now, if you're familiar with posting ads on Craigslist, then you know that they will only allow you to post one ad per email address registered with their site. To find a way around that, I set up 3 different emails to be able to re-post my ad for a "Guy and a truck needed" three more times tonight. That'll give me a total of four ads posted on their site under the labor section under three different email addresses.

Hopefully, I'll start getting some good responses. Now, we sit back and wait.

Another hour passes and nothing. *Great. You know, this might be a long shot but, let me call Eric and see what he is doing.* I haven't spoken to him in weeks due to him launching a new project and me being busy paying people back over the last few months, but it's worth a shot. I picked up my phone to give him a call. Dialed his number and he answered.

"Hello?"
"Hey, man! "I replied. "What are you up to? What are you doing right now?"
Eric says, "Nothing much. Why? What's up?"
"I picked up a gig on Craigslist to help someone move. I need a truck to do it with and you know I don't have one. Do you still have your pick-up?"
"Yeah, I got it," he said.
I get a little excited. "Can you help? I'll give you seventy-five bucks!"
"Just give me whatever it cost for gas and of course I'll help!"
I insist, "Man you're awesome. I'll give you the seventy-five for gas, cool?"
"Yeah, cool. What time do we have to be there?" he asked.
"I know this is last minute, but in two hours."

He said, "Yeah, that's fine. I'll come by your place in a few."

"Dude, you're awesome. Thanks, bro!"
"No problem."

We hang up.
I do my happy dance.
He said yes! And just like that we're in business!

I cannot believe he is available to do this! It's a Saturday night in Las Vegas and I just happen to catch him home with his truck and he's willing to help. How awesome is that? I'm so psyched. I'm going to be making fifty bucks tonight! Not to mention, I'm going to be able to go food shopping tomorrow. Dollar store, here I come! I can fill my cabinets with food for days on just thirty bucks at the dollar store. I going to eat like a king shopping for my groceries at the dollar store. I'm so excited. I get up off the floor, head out to the kitchen and go make two peanut butter sandwiches. I make two because I want to make sure that I have enough energy for tonight's move. I also won't be able to eat anything until after the move, so I better stuff my belly now. After I make my sandwiches I make my way over to the living room to sit on the couch and see what's on TV. Normally I don't watch a lot of TV, never did. When I was homeless, it was the last thing I missed, if I even missed it at all. I'm sitting on the couch because it's comfortable and not the floor in my bedroom. Sitting on the couch turns into lying on the couch, which then turns into me passing out on the couch. I guess I shouldn't have eaten both those peanut butter sandwiches so quickly. They gave me a food coma. I couldn't help it. I was hungry, but now my eyes have become ridiculously heavy and this couch is incredibly comfy. I have yet to be able to afford a bed. I wake up to my phone ringing off the hook.

It's Eric!
I hit the answer button. "What's up?"
Eric asks, "What are you doing?"
"I fell asleep."
Eric says, "OH, well, wake your ass up. I'm outside."
"Okay, thanks! I'm coming."
I rush to my bedroom to put on my only pair of shoes. I strap them up nice and tight and I'm out the door. I race down the stairs and out to his truck. I don't need him to wait a minute more, especially since he's doing me the biggest favor ever. I get to his truck, hop in and we take off.
Eric asks, "Hey! So, where are we going?"
"You're not going to believe this, but she lives right behind Summerlin Hospital, about thirty seconds from here!" I reply.

Eric says, "Nice. Where are we moving her to? What part of town?"

"Um, I have no idea...I was so happy that she booked with me that I forgot to ask."

We both laugh. I know she's moving to the other side of the valley, I just don't know where. Eric says, "Well, let's hope she isn't moving to the other side of the planet!"
I chuckle, "True."

And in minutes, we are at her gated entrance into her community. Guard gated of course. The guard asks who we are there to see. I say, "We're here to see Tanya."

The guard tells us to wait as he calls ahead to make sure. He picks up the phone and presses, what seems to me, just one number on the dial pad and suddenly, she's on the line. I looked at Eric and he can tell I'm thinking the same thing he's thinking. *They must be important people because the guard seems to have their number on speed dial.* I hear him mention my name and he then nods his head as if to say okay. He hangs up with her and motions us to continue through the gate once it's open. As soon as those gates open we are slammed by views of the hugest homes I have ever seen. Seven-million-dollar homes, easy. If the same homes we're looking at were in any other city and state, they would easily be thirteen-million-dollar homes.

Eric looks at me and says, "Who the heck are we moving?"
I respond, "I have no idea, but I do know I just made us an additional hundred bucks tip on top of the one twenty-five she already promised us! Because she can obviously afford it!"
We make a few lefts, then a right, and we end up at her house. Of course, her house fits right in. Two story homes with a three-car garage. Fresh manicured grass, palm trees and statues in the driveway. Her home is right on par with the neighboring houses, an eight-million-dollar home. These kinds of neighborhoods are the kind of neighborhoods where you find yourself living next door to celebrities who frequent Vegas so much that they decided to buy a house here. The same kind of neighborhoods that allow Eric and I to stand out like a sore thumb. We pull up and park in reverse in the driveway. I get out, put the tailgate down and go to knock on the door. As soon as I get there the door opens. It's a little girl, crystal blue eyes and tan skin, mixed race with black and white and somewhere around four years old. She's adorable.

She says, "Hi!"
"Hi!" I reply and ask if her mom is there.
"Yes!" she says and continues to stare at me. I guess my mixed features throw her off too. I ask, "Um, can you get her for me?"

"Yes!" She immediately turns and runs off, leaving the door wide open. I want to see what the inside of a millionaire home looks like, so I look around inside as I stand and wait in the doorway. I hear a mature voice start to make its way to the front door. That voice is obviously the mother by the way she's barking orders at the four-year-old. "Make sure you finish your packing, now," she commands.

She doesn't even get a chance to finish her sentence before she ends up popping out from behind the front door. I am immediately taken back. She's beautiful too. Early thirties, five-foot-nine, blue jeans, white tee, and blonde curly hair that has just been cut to shape her face. She has crystal blue eyes (now I know where her daughter got them from) and her body is well taken care of. Physically fit.

I extend my hand and before I can mention my name, she says "You're Holis, right?"

Slightly taken back by her beauty I say, "Yes, that's me." She doesn't extend her hand to shake mine, instead she looks down at mine which I still have in the air. I bring my hand down and I immediately understand how this is going to go and where she stands. Not to mention where I stand with her. There will be no fraternizing with the help here.

She turns her back to me and says, "Follow me." She motions me to come in and follow her. We take a left heading in the direction she came from. We make our way to her bedroom which is on the first floor. It looks large enough to be a master bedroom but it's downstairs. She starts to point at random items like the bed, dresser, a few boxes and says, "That's going, that's going, that's going, and that's going." She looks back at me for the first time since entering her house.

"Got it?"
I nod as if to say, *Yeah of course.*
"Good," she says and walks out of the room without saying another word. I immediately think, *she's giving me an additional hundred for this move now because I don't give a rat's ass about her being a single mom and being cute anymore, she's a straight up bitch.* She's giving me an additional $100 just out of principle alone.

Why can't people of their status ever show gratitude? Even back in the call center I worked for prior to going homeless I always made sure to thank people the people that I managed and let them know how much I appreciated and respected them for what they do, even if I didn't know them personally, even if my so-called friends at the time told me to stop because it made me look weak. I didn't care, I still did it. Anyhow, the clock is ticking, time to get to work. I head out to get Eric who is still in the driveway. We come back to the master bedroom together to get a plan in place and to start loading.

We grab the bed first. This bed is a gigantic beast. It's a custom made huge memory foam California king bed. It's amazingly large. Box spring, mattress, side skirts, headboard and footboard. All dark wood and very heavy. Geez, this move is going to take forever and Eric's going to hate me when we're done. After only what I can assume was five minutes, she makes her way back into the bedroom to check on our progress.

I take this time to ask her,
"Was this bed custom-made? It's impressively huge!"
Tanya replies while pointing at her four-year-old,
"Yes, her father is over seven feet tall."
I jokingly say, "Wow, over seven feet tall! What basketball team does he play for and can I get an autograph?"
She doesn't answer. Instead she turns her back to us, walks out of the room and just as she's disappearing says, "Tick tock, the clock is ticking. Lets get a move on!"

After what felt like two hours we eventually get everything loaded up in the back of Eric's truck. The bed, the dresser, and the few boxes all barely fit in the back of his truck. They're either placed in the bed or in the crew cab and just like that, Eric's Dodge Ram crew cab with an eight-foot bed, is all out of space. We couldn't take another box even if we wanted to. I go inside to do one more walk-through to make sure we got everything. I meet her in the room, and it looks like she was doing the same in other parts of the house. I tell her that we are all packed up and ready to go.

"Good," she says.
"I'll meet you outside. I have to lock up and set the security alarm."

I head outside and hop in the truck. We wait. We wait for about fifteen minutes before she finally comes out. *I guess we're on her time now?* She walks past the passenger side of the truck and in one breath she says once again, "Follow me." No directions. You'd think she would say, *"This is where we are going, do you know how to get there?"* but nope, nothing. Again, I get the impression that the hired help is on a need to know basis.

She hops into her SUV which just so happens to match her attitude towards life, ugly…and we're off. We exit out of her community, make our way down a few major roads and out on to the highway. As we drive, Eric and I start to come up with scenarios of why she's moving and why she only took a bedroom set versus the rest of the house. Eric's hypothesis is that she's moving because she found a better job and decided to move closer to work. I'm not buying that for a second. My guess is that she's the daughter of very rich parents, daddy's little girl went out to a nightclub one night, met a black guy, liked him, kept seeing her black boyfriend without telling Daddy. She got pregnant, had her daughter, now daddy can't forgive his little princess for dating a black guy, so he kicks her and the grandchild out. And no, that wasn't racist. Maybe her father is, it's just my hypothesis. How else would you explain her move and her mixed daughter?
Forty-five minutes goes by and we're still driving. What the hell?
Eric finally asks, "Where the heck are we going?"

I look at the road signs. "Did we just pass Green Valley Ranch?"
"Yes! This is far and I'm burning up a lot of gas," Eric declares

I pick up my phone and call her. She answers.

Tanya: "Yes?"
I try one more time to crack a joke. "Hey, If I knew we were going to Mexico I would have packed my passport!"

She laughs. Finally, a sign that shows that she is a real person with real emotions.

Then she says, "We're going to the Wagon Wheel exit. It's the next exit."
I ask, "Where?"
Tanya says, "Just follow me. We'll be there in ten minutes."
"Okay."

We hang up.

After a few minutes and a couple of passed exits we end up at the very last exit in Nevada before hitting what feels like the Arizona state line. *Are you kidding me?* We take the Wagon Wheel exit, take a few turns and end up at a brand-new apartment complex. It's a far cry from where we just left an hour ago. I don't see any gated entrances or guards. I don't see any multi-million-dollar homes out here. Not one manicured lawn. No trimmed palm trees. Not to mention, there are average cars in the parking lot. *What's going on here?* We get to her building. We park, and she walks me to her apartment. We make it to her front door and she opens it up. I step into what is a far cry from her house we just moved her from. She was living in a pristine mansion with grandiose furniture and what looked like expensive artwork hanging from the walls, to her new apartment that could not be any more than nine hundred square feet. A two bed one bath, typical Vegas apartment, but what caught my attention was not the size but the condition of the apartment. It looks like she's being living here with her daughter for a few weeks now. It looks like a crash pad, or like squatters have been living in here. I mean, this place is a mess. Crap, garbage, left over pizza boxes and kids toys are scattered everywhere and a sleeping blanket laid out in what should be the living room. I can't believe that her and her daughter, before we moved their bedroom set tonight, have been sleeping on the floor in this mess. My heart breaks. She points to where a dining room table should go and says, "You can put the bed there and the dresser can go in the bedroom." I feel incredibly bad for coming to the conclusion that I did for the reason she was moving because that's obviously not the case, the case is, she's obviously going through some shit.

I was going to hit her up for an extra hundred for this move and it would have been justified with how long we've been on this job coupled with how far we drove to get her stuff here, but after seeing how she's living, I can't do that now. Not to mention, this hits home hard for me because I'm sleeping on the floor at my place as well right now and I don't have a daughter sleeping next to. I can't help but feel like we should do something about this. I have no idea why she moved out of a clean mansion to live here, in her two-bedroom apartment that is covered in trash, but Eric and I are going to do something about this. I head out to the Eric's truck and update him, prepare him, for what he's about to walk into.

I say to him, "Dude, I'm *not* hitting her up for an extra hundred and that I'll explain later. Also, do *not* make any funny faces or say anything about their living condition once inside either. It's obviously none of our business and out of respect for her and her daughter, let's put the bed together for her and her daughter once we get it unloaded. Cool?"

He looks at me like I'm crazy.

"Did you forget about our conversations in the truck and how she treated us back at her old house?"
I reply, "I remember, but everything is different now. I'll explain later. Let's just get everything unloaded."

He nods and agrees to go ahead and set up her bed with me so that they both have a soft surface to sleep on tonight. It's funny, just an hour ago I couldn't stand her. Now I'm going above and beyond to make sure she's set up with somewhere for her and her daughter to sleep tonight. Funny how life is crazy that way.

We unload the bed and make our way into her apartment. Eric carrying one side and myself carrying the other. We walk in and make our way toward her bedroom. Eric does his best to keep his promise and not say anything or making any weird faces as he gets a glimpse of what I was talking about.

She stops us half way through the living room and says, "Where are you going? I said to just leave the bed in the dining room."

I say, "We've decided to set up the bed for you so that you and your daughter both have somewhere to sleep tonight."

This bed is so big that I can't see her and it's almost falling out of my hands in front of me. Then I think I hear her sniffle, as if she just started to cry. Not sure why. It's not like I was just going to leave her here to put this massive bed together on her own. Her silence only tells me that she likes the gesture and that it's okay to keep going towards the bedroom. Eric and I keep going and finally make it to her bedroom, which is no different from the living room. Small and trashed with kid's toys and garbage everywhere. We clear some trash out of the way to set her bed up. We head out to the truck to get some tools and the rest of her stuff. Luckily, Eric had some tools in his truck. He learned to keep them on him wherever he goes because his truck would turn off and not want to turn back on often.

His truck is not that reliable, but hey, it got us here, plus it's putting fifty bucks in my pocket so that I can do some food shopping after this move. While Eric plays around with his tools to find the right ones for the job, I grab the rest of the boxes that are left in the crew cab. We lock up the truck and carry the rest her belongings inside.

Twenty-five minutes later, her bed is put back together, and she is finally moved. We make our way out to the living room to get paid and get ready to say goodbye. We talk while her daughter plays, and she thanks us. I tell her about how I used to work for a call center and that I am now getting back on my feet as well. It's almost like the person I met back in Summerlin three hours ago was her evil twin or something, because she's completely humbled right now and showing us a ton of gratitude. I'm sure seeing her place in its current condition as outsiders for the first time does open her up to being vulnerable. I'm sure that a certain level of unspoken respect and trust amongst the three of us was created because of the way that we handled it, too. I'm pleased to have helped her move, and glad that she chose me to move her.

She hugs me and finally, for the first time tonight, extends her hand to shake mine. I immediately feel something that feels like cash slide into my palm. Cash in the palm of your hands is always a good thing. To show her respect, I don't count it. I just place it in my pocket and hug her again and make my way toward the front door. Before I'm completely out of the front door I hear, "Hey!" It's her four-year-old.

I turn back into the apartment and she's right behind me. I say, "Yes, my love?" Tanya's daughter says, "I like you mister!"

She gives me the same hand shake her mom gave me. Funny how kids never miss a step. No money in my palm of my hands this time, but I did get the approval from a four-year-old, and you can't pay for that kind of childlike honesty.

Eric and I exit. We make our way back to the truck, exhausted. We get in and I take the time I reach in my pocket to count how much she gave us. It's $125 even. After seeing her apartment, I didn't expect for her to give us any more than that. I give Eric his share, seventy-five bucks. He takes it, he deserves it, and together we call it a night.

We make our way back to the highway and finally start our long journey back to the Vegas valley. Then my phone rings.
It's Tanya. I ask, "Hey, did we forget to unload something?" I look around the truck and don't see anything that we forgot to unload.
Tanya says, "No you guys moved everything. You guys were great and thank you again."
"Sure!" I say. For a while, there is silence.
"So, what's up?"
"You mentioned that you were a concierge once here, right?" she asks.
"Was, yeah. Why?"

Tanya says, "So does that mean you have connections all over the city?"
"Well, it's been a while and I've gone through some life changes, but for the most part, yeah. I'm sure it wouldn't take long to get back in touch with those same contacts. Why do you ask?"
"This might seem like a weird request, granted that I just met you two, but do you think you can get something for me?"
I'm puzzled. "Get something for you?"
"Yes, like...drugs?"
I'm stunned. "Oh, yeah. I don't think..."
She cuts me off.
"Speed. I'm looking for speed…"
"You want me to find you speed?" I ask.
"Yes!"
Well, I guess now we know the real reason why she got kicked out of her parents' mansion. Dad wasn't upset because she was supposedly dated a black guy and got pregnant, Dad's upset because his daughter has a drugs problem and she's about to tempt me like I've never been tempted before.

CHAPTER TWENTY-ONE

Lead me not into temptation

CHAPTER TWENTY-ONE

Lead me not into temptation

"I'LL CALL YOU BACK."

I press the hang-up button. I slowly move my phone away from my ear and watch it drop to my knee. I look over at Eric.

"Bro, you know the single mom we just moved, Tanya."
Eric nods. "Yeah."
"She just called me back, and you have no idea what she just asked me for."
Eric says sarcastically, "She likes you and asked if you would like to come back for a quickie?"
I chuckle, "That would be nice since it's been a while, but no."
Eric suggests, "She's an escort and wants fifty dolla to make you holla?"
"No, but seriously. I told her that I used to be a concierge back in the day and that I used to have hook-ups all over the city."
"Okay," he says.

"She wants to know if I can get her drugs."
Eric shrugs. "What's wrong with that?"
"First, I'm not a drug dealer, and secondly, she doesn't want the simple stuff like weed, she wants real shit."
"What's real shit?" he asks.
"She wants speed!"
"Oh, that's some fucked up stuff."
I sigh, "I know. I've never been asked that question before."

We both go silent. Nothing is said, simply because I think he smokes weed, but most importantly he knows that I don't do drugs at all. To each their own, but I could care less for them. I was always the kid in high school who didn't smoke weed but liked the smell of it and didn't mind being around it. It starts to become an even longer car ride home now. In the quietness of the ride I try to come to some sort of a decision in my head. After all, she is waiting for me to call her back.

Now, I know what you're thinking. *What is there to think about? She's a single mom who's a drug addict and the money she should be spending on her daughter she's spending on drugs. Whoever supplies her with her drugs is a downright loser and that's not you!*

The problem is, when you find yourself in the position that I am in, you start thinking twice about everything. When you are hungry, and you have no idea where your next meal is going to come from, you start to see that the lines of right and wrong start to crisscross. To become blurry. You can justify doing something wrong if it means you'll be able to eat tonight. Some people might say that digging in the garbage for food is wrong, but I've done it. You'll be surprised at what you will do when you're hungry. Do the wrong thing and eat, or do the right thing and die starving? It really becomes that black and white when you've been stripped of everything you've ever owned, loved, believed in, and now must live life based on your survival instincts like a wild animal.

I start to think about my refrigerator back home. I start to think about how empty it is. I start to think about how empty my cabinets are. I start to think of how much food I could fill them with from the profits of doing this one deal! But, you know they're not called drug dealers because they've only sold one drug once. They usually never get into the game of selling drugs just to sell one drug to one person once. I start to ask myself, *how much does speed sell for anyways? How much could I buy it for, wholesale? How much could I sell it for retail? What about just below retail?* The right price, the right product could keep her coming back religiously. *What's the difference between good premium Speed and crap Speed? Who could I call? Where would I get it from?* I can't help it. I don't see drugs at this point. I see supply, demand, a means to an end to fill my empty fridge and the funds to be able to see my boy next weekend.

Yeah, but you just got fifty bucks in your pocket, Holis.
Yeah, but I can potentially get an additional three hundred in my pocket if I do this!

After all, this is something that I'm used to doing, meeting supply with demand. When I was a concierge in Las Vegas back in the day for me was all about supply and demand.

When my friends were visiting here they needed a service like mine (the demand) so I gave it to them for a fee (the supply.) At that time, there were just two other people in Las Vegas providing a concierge service, that's it. So, there was a lot of demand for what we provided. When people needed to know where the best nightclub was at on a Saturday, they called me. When they wanted into the hottest pool party on a Sunday, they called me. I got them in, got a fee for getting them in the hottest pool parties, and then I moved on to the next customer. So how is this any different?

Ultimately my connections and knowledge of the city became the supply that I filled my demand with. I became exclusive with my connections and who I worked with, and as a result, my clients became exclusive, too. Real high-end clients who ate, breathed, and lived the slogan, "What happens in Vegas stays in Vegas". They would come into town and religiously ask the same four things: girls, a table with bottle service in one of the hardest clubs to get into, occasionally food, and drugs. The most popular drugs were coke, ecstasy, pills and marijuana. No matter who it was, a judge, a lawyer, a big wig CEO, a celebrity or regular guy from Nebraska, my answer was always the same. "You know that I am your concierge. I do not work for the casinos, I work for you. What I will do is I will get you into the private rooms inside the walls at the MGM for ten grand hands of blackjack, no problem. A chef's table at the most exclusive restaurant in Las Vegas that currently has a three-month wait list, no problem. I can even get you a private villa overlooking Elton's Vegas mansion, no problem. What I will NOT get you is simple. Two things. I will never get you a prostitute, and I will never get you drugs. You want that, go contact your local level casino host who has no morals or standards."

Believe it or not, even though they'd get upset, for the most part, this answer gained respect and I ended up retaining more clients than not. That was during a time when I had clout and when I had a client book the size of California so, I could care less if I lost a client with a prostitute and coke problem.

Now, times are bad. I'm not loner in that business (obviously), I have no money, no one even knows me, my client book doesn't exist, and I've been eating out of garbage cans. So, like I said, I'm contemplating everything right now. With all the contemplating that I have been doing on this car ride home, and the questions that I have been pondering I failed to notice how much time has slipped away. I get a text. It's Tanya. *So, are you able to get me what I asked for?*

I look up at Eric for the second time during this car ride and ask," What do you think? She's asking for an update, if I can get it." Eric says, "Well, can you get it?" "I have no idea, but if anyone can get it, I know one guy that I can call. He's connected to everything in that world. He knew who I was and approached me once at the club to solicit me his business once. He was and at that time had been trying to get my clients to buy from him for years."

Eric then tells me, "I don't know if you know this, but did you know just having that stuff on you is considered possession, and is 10 years in jail?"
Eric was always good about knowing random true facts about almost everything and anything, including the law.

I'm aghast. "What? No!"
He insists, "Yes!"
I chuckle, "Oh fuck that! Have you seen my face? I'd make a pretty boyfriend in jail!"

We both laugh, but in all seriousness, his threat only slowed me down. I'm still thinking about doing it.

I text her back: *I'm working on it!*
She texts: *OK, let me know asap.*

Why didn't I just tell her that I cannot do it? Why don't I just walk away before I really get myself in trouble? It's the temptation of easy money. Remember, I just lost my job. My refrigerator and my stomach are both still empty and this easy money would be a great way to solve both of those problems.

"Fuck it! I'm calling the guy from the club." I think his name is Ben. Let me see how much this stuff goes for, anyway. I go to my contacts in my phone and type in Ben in the search bar and what do you know? He's the only Ben I have saved in my phone. I know it's him because I added the word "doctor" after his name in my contacts to remind me of his profession. Obviously, he's not a family doctor. He does offer what doctors offer though...drugs. I press the call button.

He answers.
"Hello?"
"Ben?" I ask.
"Who's this?"
"It's Holis, Las Vegas Concierge. You met me at the club a few years back."
His voice cheers up. "Oh yeah! Mr. G5's, I remember you. What's up brotha? How's the high-end concierge business?"

"It's okay I guess, as a matter of fact I'm no longer in it. How are you?" He says, "I'm good bro, doing what I do, you know! What's the deal? What can I do you for?"
"I have a friend in town and she's lost."

This is where the conversation goes cryptic and where I hope he follows me enough to remain on the same page during this conversation.

"Lost?" he says. "What is she looking for?"
"A movie but I forget the name. She's looking for that movie, the one with Keanu Reeves and Sandra Bullock." (Insert drug that I am looking for here.)
Ben says, "Oh wow! Yeah, exactly, I remember that movie!"

(Yep, I believe we are on the same page.)

I continue, "By the way, remember part two when they did the same concept on a cruise ship?"

"Yeah, I remember that one," he says.
"How much do those cruise tickets go for anyways?"
(How much does a bag of speed go for?)
Ben offers, "Depends if you're traveling alone or with a friend."

(How many bags are you looking for?)
I say, "Alone."
(Just 1 bag.)
Ben thinks for a second. "Don't know, but I believe those cruise tickets can range anywhere from a hundred to one hundred and fifty bucks per ticket."
"What about a room with a view the boat, what do you think that goes for?"
(I'm asking for the good stuff right now, premium shit.)
Ben: "One fifty a ticket. Definitely one fifty."
"Oh, that's pretty cheap ticket for a cruise."
(Pretty good price for premium shit.)
I decide to ask, "Also, I heard that if you get caught with a fake cruise line ticket, that you can get locked up for ten years?"
(I heard that if you get caught with just one bag that you can go to jail for ten years.)
Ben agrees. "I've heard the same."
I say, "Damn. Alright man, well never mind. My friend just sent me a text and said she found her ticket. I'll talk to later."
(The deal is off. Ten years is no joke.)
Ben replies, "It's all good. Holla whenever."

We both hang up.

I look back at Eric. We basically just pulled up to my apartment complex and I tell him exactly what I am thinking. "Fuck that!" Before we pull up to my building I send Tanya a text: *Nope, I will not be able to get that for you.*

She responds back instantly: *I appreciate you trying. I am leaving for California this weekend and will be back in Vegas next week. I will text you when I get back to see if anything has changed.*

In my head I'm thinking, *Bitch are you crazy? I'm not selling you shit!* In my text: *Yeah, I don't think anything will have changed in between now and next week*. She doesn't respond back. I don't think she liked my last text.

We pull up to my building and Eric puts his truck in park. He extends his hand for a quick handshake and I oblige.

Eric says, "Well, it sure has been an adventure."
I chuckle, "I know, right? You've gotta love Craigslist."
"I have to get going, but if you need anything tomorrow just shoot me a text" he offers.
I smile at him. "For sure. Thanks again for all your help. You helped me put fifty bucks in my pocket tonight."
"My pleasure."

The entire time he's probably thinking to himself, *I have no idea who you were just talking to and why you were talking about going on a cruise but whatever!* We finish shaking hands and I hop out. I close the door behind me and hear him put his car in drive and pull away. I make my way to my building and head up my stairs. I can't help but wonder, *how much money could I have made on tonight if it did go through?* Immediately the smarter side of my brain kicks in with its answer. *Ten years Holis. Ten years.* Yep, not worth it. Well, at least I'm fifty dollars richer and I didn't have to rob anyone or sell any drugs to get it. I'll be able to buy a loaf of bread, some jelly to match my peanut butter in my fridge and a gallon of water in the morning and feel good about where the money came from when I do spend it.

Funny thing is, I guess even when you are this broke that the lines between good and evil really aren't as blurred as I thought. At the end of the day it all comes down to decisions. See, we all have a choice to make and when the easy way comes knocking, we can either answer the temptation or turn around and walk away pretending we never heard temptation knock in the first place.

I might not be thinking correctly sometimes because of my situation, but if I continue to make the right decisions like I did tonight, I just might find my path. Now, let's go upstairs and check the garbage for dinner and see what my roommate has thrown out that's still good to eat. We'll call that a night and head off to bed. For tomorrow is a new day.

CHAPTER TWENTY-TWO
I'm not going anywhere

CHAPTER TWENTY-TWO

I'm not going anywhere

I MUST ADMIT, when it comes to writing in you journal, I've been ignoring you lately and I'm sorry. That's only because I've incredibly been busy with moving people and looking for jobs on Craigslist. When it comes to booking moves, I think that I might have cracked the code to winning moving bids on CL. Not to mention, the last moving gig I got, I had gotten lucky. The owners were moving out of their house in a rush, the kind of rush move that looks like 'We're avoiding a forceful eviction' kind of move (Been through one—sorry, two in the last months if you count the abandoned office I was sleeping in.)

And I think that it was a 'avoiding a forceful eviction' kind of move because I know all too well what they look, smell, and taste like. I can feel exactly what they (the people who I moved) are going through and how they're feeling. I know exactly what they were experiencing emotionally and physically. I know all about the vein-popping-out-of-your-forehead-type fights that lead up to that night.

Every hurtful, deceitful, below-the-belt words, the curses that are so ear piercing that they're just as damaging as the words themselves. Eviction is never a happy thing and if you have a life partner coming along for the ride, it's never going to end well. I know it all and I kept it to myself as I moved them.

None of my business, and as a matter of fact, I'm just here to move them for a mere seventy-five bucks. After all, I've got my own problems to work out and I'm also moving them on an empty stomach. So, how about we start picking up our feet, folks!

We begin to move their stuff, and as soon as we do I quickly notice that I am the only one here to help them move. They mentioned that there were supposed to be another three guys coming to help, but I guess they didn't get the memo. This is a four-bedroom house full of armoires, living room sets, bedroom sets, dressers, and stairs. These guys better show up because if they don't I'm going to be here for five hours moving easy. This isn't looking good for me. If these other guys don't show up, he better do a lot better than seventy-five bucks to help him move or I'm going to be pissed. We get started and, of course, it's just the husband and myself. *And*, no offense, but this guy doesn't look like he's going to be much help at all. First, he can't go twenty feet without lighting up another cigarette and taking a break. He's already had three energy drinks and it's only been an hour. He's in his forties and he looks like the last time he saw a gym, he drove past it, six years ago.

I'm not judging, I'm just a little annoyed that the other guys didn't show up and now I'm moving this four-bedroom house by myself, with a guy that looks like he eats honey buns for breakfast. The last thing I need is for this guy to give out on me while I'm carrying his heavy ass dresser down the stairs with me navigating from the bottom.

We end up moving everything that wasn't nailed down to the ground. He even had crap outside that he wanted to take with him. Folding sun chairs, a water hose, a few plant pots. Like, really? Is that water hose that priceless to you that you have to pack it up and bring it with you? Like you can't get another one at Home Depot for fourteen dollars anytime soon? Anyhow, five hours later (I originally thought four) and we finally get him moved. My fingers are swollen, I'm sweating, and my back hurts. From this point on, before I agree to any more moves my first question is going to be "How many rooms are you moving?" and "How much are you paying?" The same questions I would ask when I worked over the phones at my old moving job. It never made sense to me why they made us ask those questions until now. The good news is that we didn't take any of the *real* heavy stuff, like the fridge or the stove, but we still moved enough heavy stuff to fill his twenty-three-foot U-Haul truck that he rented.

The sad news is, from what I recognized while doing this move, it looks like this couple won't be making it through this eviction or move together. Most couples when they move will mark their boxes with "living room" or "bedroom" labels. This couple has marked their boxes with "mine" and/or "his stuff." Just the fact alone that his girlfriend, or wife, would mark his boxes with "his stuff" shows that she's a little bitter and that she has no plans to stay with him after this move. Pissed off might be a better word. Even worse, it looks like she might be taking their kid with her, too. It's sad because we'd like to think that "we" as a couple could make it through anything if you have love. Sometimes, as I know firsthand, love just isn't enough.

Five hours later we're done. I'm sweating, I'm hurting, and he's literally sweating through his shirt and completely out of breath. Thank God for my conditioning from doing these moves or I would be just as out of breath as this guy is. I'm smiling inside because he gave it his best. You should admire the guy. He's a hard worker when he wants to be. He deserves a hug, not just for the hard work that he's put in, but for the strength that he's showing going through what he is going through with his family. His hug isn't coming from me though, that's for sure. He's too damn sweaty. He walks over (please no hugs) and hands me an envelope.

I can tell that there is money inside. He says, "Thanks for helping me move today, and for not quitting on me when at any time you could have." Me quit? Not after what I've been through.

I reply "No problem. I hope that you get to where you're going. Not just with this move but in life, even if it's by yourself."

He nods with approval. My attention is back on the envelope that he gave me and I've become so excited to have money that I open it immediately right in front of him. Bad manners, I know, but I allow my excitement to get the best of me. I open it to find out very quickly that after five hours of packing and moving his four-bedroom house, this guy has the nerve to hand me an envelope with a mere fifty-dollar bill in it.

Sigh.
I look up at him and ask, "Really?" "Come on man."

Why does this keep happening to me? I looked down into the envelope, I look up at him again, and he has this look on his face like he wasn't expecting me to open the envelope right in front of him. I bring my hands up shoulder length and make the gesture, *So what's the deal?* Before I can say anything he, let's call him Danny, says, "I'm sorry, but it is all I have. I know you worked hard and I appreciate it but, I have nothing else to give." I retort, "You promised me seventy-five dollars for this move!" Danny winces. "I know. My baby girl needs formula and my wife is on my ass about not having a job or enough money to move into our new placc. It's all I got."

"Listen, everyone goes through problems in their lives. Believe me, I know! I was just in your same situation just a few months ago, literally, but this is bullshit," I say. "You obviously have more than this because you were planning on paying three of us to do this move with you."
Danny just looks down at the ground and stays completely silent.

I growl, "I'm not going to get any more money than this, am I?" Danny is again silent.
I ask, "If that was the case, why not be that honest with me upfront? Knowing your situation, I probably would have moved you anyways."

Danny only agrees with a head nod.
"So, what do we do?" I ask.

Danny doesn't say anything.

In his silence, I immediately look around to see what I can take in exchange for what he owes me. Anything of cash value that I can sell to make up for the money that he promised me from the very beginning.

This is frustrating. You do good things for people and sometimes they just let you down. One thing is for sure, I'm not leaving here without something to make up for the remaining $25 he owes me. I mean, I busted my ass working for this guy. It's just not fair. We had a deal and at the last minute, he's trying to get over on me.

Remember, he's shorted me twenty-five bucks and I still have to pay my ride from Craigslist forty bucks to pick me up here and drop me off back at home. I didn't come help this guy move *for five hours* for a mere ten dollars!

Just as I'm done scanning over all the objects being left behind in the open garage, I notice her. There she was, the queen bed I remembered from the spare bedroom. We had carried it down the stairs because his wife wanted to take it with her, but soon changed her mind to be able to fit more of the baby's room onto the truck. He looks at me and then looks at it. He notices me staring at it.

Danny offers, "Why don't you take it with you? If you want it, it's yours."
I reply, "Are you serious? It's practically brand new."
Happiness returns back to his face, "Yeah, we got it for her mom but when things started to go bad with us, her mom stopped visiting. She barely used it."
"Are you sure, though?"

Danny replies, "Of course! Let's be honest, I owe you a lot more than just twenty-five bucks, moving this entire house just the two of us."
I smile at him. "You're right, you do, and I'll take it! You got yourself a deal!"

I guess sometimes people can also surprise you too, in a good way. I'm already imagining falling asleep on it, and just like that I'm no longer sleeping on the floor in my own bedroom. I've officially became the owner of a new bed, and it's in great condition, too! I'm feeling elated right now! Getting it home, though, is going to be a different story. My rideshare drives a compact car and has no idea that I'm bringing a bed home with me.

I text my rides and bring her up to speed. I let her know that I'm done, that I'm ready to be picked up, and that I will be bringing a new bed back with me. Graciously, she said, "*No problem, we can strap it to the roof. Be there in 20!*" I don't know what it is, but deep down, I can feel my luck starting to change, and as weird as it might sound, it's all because of this move and my new bed. This is going to be the first bed I've slept in since going homeless and I cannot wait to try it out tonight.

My rideshare gets here and we strap my new queen bed and box spring to her roof. Thanks to the ratchet straps that the guy I just moved has given me, she (my new bed) won't be going anywhere anytime soon. We eventually get the bed to my house. It's not heavy and after moving all day, it's almost like I got a second wind because I was able to carry my new bed and box spring up my stairs without any help at all. My ride takes off after I give her the forty bucks that I owe her for picking me up and for returning me home after this move. As soon as she takes off, I go to my bedroom to admire my new bed. Finally, after a month, my bedroom is starting to come together. Finally, she's starting to resemble something of a real room.

I cover her with a blanket, the one and only blanket that I had the whole time since I have gone homeless. I lay down on my bed and it must have been a combination of working in the sun today, moving this guy, and the feeling of being back on a bed because in seconds, immediately I fall asleep. I slept so well. I slept like a baby. It's amazing, you'll be surprised at the little things that we all take for granted.

Since that move I haven't had that many moves off Craigslist, so I've devoted most of my time to submitting resumes online. I must find a real source of income that I can count on, because the holidays are coming, and I want to give my boy the best Christmas ever. To do that, I'm going to need more than just seventy-five-dollar moves once or twice a week. I've made it my mission to find a new job in two weeks. I've got my fingers crossed, my goal of finding a good paying job written down with a due date, and I'm not making any excuses. It's go time.

Since waking up from my glorious nap, I've submitted my resume to about fifty job listings online (no lie) and heard back from a handful of them that want to interview me next week. One of them is with a company that makes mobile apps for businesses. Sounds interesting, but I've been on plenty of interviews over the past month and after wasting my time, almost all of them were commission-only jobs. Jobs that were multi-level marketing "opportunities" or fly-by-night call centers. I've just worked for one that was legit up until the point when you hit the commission scale. Once you did, they'd pull the rug out from underneath you and keep all your commission. So, yeah, after that, my defenses are up and I'm not one-bit hopeful that any of these will pan out. We will see.

The good news is that my ex has been making it easy for me to see my son. Don't ask me how, but with every ten dollars I make, I give her five, even if it means I go without eating until my next move. The last time I couldn't afford to eat I was homeless. This time I have a roof over my head and a bed, so one could say I'm ahead of the game. When it comes to giving her what I can when I can, I'm at least able to help to do my share, even if it's not a lot. I've paid for his daycare, diapers, and food. Don't get me wrong, she takes her parting shots from time to time to remind me of how much of a loser I am, and that I'm not a good father, but I guess that's how the game goes. For the most part though, we agree to disagree. I don't know too many people that have gone through what I've been through. From going homeless, eating out of garbage cans and dumpsters, from sleeping on the streets and abandoned offices, only to get back on their feet without a drug addiction or alcohol challenge. Just to finally say "I'm back!" ...

But I can.

CHAPTER TWENTY-THREE

Rollercoasters and life

CHAPTER TWENTY-THREE
Rollercoasters and life

THE WEEKEND COMES AND GOES by quickly now that I have a real bed and have been getting real sleep. Many thanks to the guy that I moved this weekend. He may have shorted me twenty-five bucks after I helped him move, but he made up for it by giving me a seven-hundred-dollar, nearly new, barely broken in bed. I don't think I've slept this well in years. I wasn't sleeping well at all when I was sleeping on the ground. Sometimes at night, I swear I can hear my bed talking to me, "*Come to me,*" I picture my bed saying. I kindly oblige, every time for a restful night sleep. Never fails.

I must've passed out in bed by nine p.m. both Saturday and Sunday, and woke up by four am just because my bed won't stop calling me. This is a good thing, because being up by four allows me to wake up early and get started on my sixty-minute walks before the rest of the Vegas valley wakes up. While others are just getting home from last night's debauchery, I'm exiting my house to go for a walk. Even though I'm no longer working, I'm still doing my best to stay disciplined and to keep the promises that I've made to myself to never go back to being homeless ever again.

Monday has come and gone as well because I am so excited for my interviews that I have lined up today. I originally had three interviews lined up, but after some quick research, I found that one of them was a call center that paid commission only. I won't be going to that interview. I do have two other interviews and they both look pretty good. Both look like legit companies so far, with legit hourly salaries. They also have pretty good websites and an 800 number where the operator answers every time. I know because I've called both them, twice. I also called Eric yesterday. As much as I hate leaning on him for rides, I had to. I don't have enough money to pay forty-bucks to a ride-share for a trip to and from these interviews today. Plus, to be completely honest, I like riding with Eric. I can give him $20 for gas, get him a meal off the dollar menu and we're even Steven. Even if I can't afford to eat with him, I know that at least he'll be happy. He has a thing for their double cheese burgers. As long as I've known him, he's always enjoyed fast food.

It's Tuesday. Interview day and I've made my way back from my morning walk in record time. I take a shower, get dressed, and make something to eat in the kitchen.

My first interview isn't until 9:30 and I'm not expecting Eric to be here until 8:30. Since I have time to kill, I've decided to go online and continue to post and submit my resume to available job postings. I only have two interviews today. I don't have a job yet, so I must keep pushing forward no matter what. I probably submit my resume to about thirteen different job postings before my text message alert on my phone goes off.

It's Eric. *Be there in 15.*

Man, I cannot tell you how much I love this guy right now. It's amazing, but with everything that I have been through, he has consistently been there for me. I don't know why, but he has. One day I'm going to pay him back for everything that he's done for me, big time. I submit my resume to about four more positions available online when my text alert goes off again.

It's Eric: *I'm here.*

I immediately say to myself, *What? Fifteen minutes went by that fast?*

I grab my shoes, my keys, and make my way out the door as fast as possible. The last thing I want him to do is wait for me outside after he's taken his morning off to give me rides, once again, to these two interviews.

I make my way down my stairs from my second-floor apartment, down the walkway and out to the parking lot, but this time I don't see him. I look left and right, and I see nothing. I don't see his typical work truck. Just as I'm about to dig in my pocket to pull out my phone to call and ask him where he's at, I hear a car horn beep once. I look over in the direction of the sound of the horn and it's Eric…in a car I've never seen him in before.

It's an older four-door sedan, maroon. It's small and has seen better days. I walk over, and he unlocks the doors, and I get in. I'm surprised that they open automatically.

I ask him, "Bro, whose car is this? Where did you get this piece of shit from?"
Eric says, "It's my Mom's."
I wince. "Oh, just let me know when it's okay to take my foot back out of my mouth?"

"Hey, this piece of shit is getting you back and forth to your interviews today, so..."

"No seriously, my bad, I'm sorry. I had no idea." I say.

Eric laughs. "I'm just fucking with you. This car has been in the family a long time and everyone in the family already knows it's a piece of shit."

We both laugh. Just like that, we are off to my first interview of the day.

It's funny. As we talk I start to notice that something inside me is different. I can feel it. There's a certain calm has come over me that I've never felt before. I'm not as frightened, nervous, or scared as I was the first time around when I was looking for work after shooting straight out of being homeless. It's almost as if I could care less if I get these jobs or not. For some reason, I know that even if I only have lint in my pocket instead of cash that I will be alright.

I'm not nervous one bit. I look down at my hands and it's a miracle they're not all sweaty. It's a miracle because whenever I get nervous, a sure way to tell is if my hands are sweaty, and right now they aren't. It's crazy.

We get to my first interview. Turning into the parking lot I've noticed that the building is huge. Probably seventeen floors, all glass, and they have a nice corporate style grassy knoll out in front of the building with picnic tables where you can eat lunch outside if the day calls for it. We're here early. It's exactly 9:05 a.m. and I'm not supposed to be here until 9:30 a.m. I make my way out of Eric's mom's piece-of-shit car (that still got me here) and make my way into the building. I'm impressed. This building has marble floors. Nice dark wood features and pictures on the walls in the hallways of Las Vegas mayors who've come and gone, including our current one. Okay, so maybe the sweaty hands are going to make an appearance after all. I feel them starting to become clammy. This might be the job and the opportunity I've been waiting for. I push the button for the elevator to return to the first floor and as soon as it does, I hop in and make my way up to the fifteenth floor. The elevator opens and immediately I'm in the lobby of the company that called me here for an interview. Their lobby, as you would expect it, is exceptionally clean and impeccably decorated. High end furniture and glass everywhere with a pop of red color here and a pop yellow color there. Something that you would find in an exclusive luxury decor magazine.

Even my first breath of fresh air as I stepped out of the elevator and into their lobby was crisp and clean. This place is definitely a far cry from where I was just a month ago. I spot the secretary, a beautiful twenty-something brunette with eye glasses on that were obviously meant for fashion and not for vision. As I make my way over to her, I also notice there aren't a bunch of people lined up in the lobby wearing suits. Could it be that they're selective with whom they bring in for interviews? No massive hiring sprees here. Not like the other companies that I've interviewed for before I found the moving job. I hope this company is as good as it looks right now. I mention to her who I am here to see and in her sweet, sultry, and almost innocent voice, she writes down my name and lets me know that he will be with me in a minute. I thank her, turn, and take a seat.

Now, just past her desk from where I am sitting, I can see the sales floor. It's an open floor plan and I can see roughly six to seven reps at any given time walking to and from their desks. Getting up out of their desks with papers and not returning with them when they return. Sales slips perhaps? I also notice that everyone who walks by is dressed for business. Not business casual but for *business*. Ties on the men and the women are wearing long skirts and power suits. My next thought is, *I hope that they will accept me in my business casual clothing for the next weeks or so until I get my first paycheck, because I don't own any of those types of clothing.* Just as I can finish that thought, my interviewer Brad makes his way around the corner, walks over and introduces himself to me. Brad is in his early thirties and on the heavy side but walks like he knowns his shit and possibly has an important role here where he makes big decisions. He makes his way to where I am sitting and extends his hand out for a handshake. "Holis, I presume."

I smile and shake his hand. "Yes!"
"My name is Brad. Nice to meet you. I'll be the one interviewing you today. Why don't you follow me, and we can officially get started?"
I nod. "Sure."

We make our way past receptionist and walk out to the sales floor. My first thought is not that of the sales floor, but of how amazing people treat you when they know you've showered, and that you probably have a place of residence. We make our way past the sales floor to an executive conference room, again all glass and dark wood, just like the lobby. There is one large flat screen TV on the wall, perfect for video conference calls, and the chairs here are impressive. They are large, made of leather and extremely comfy.

Brad points to one of the chairs. "Here, take a seat."

As soon as I sit down I'm thinking, *I really hope this interview doesn't take too long because I could fall asleep sitting straight up in these chairs if it does. That's how nice these chairs are.* We officially begin our interview.

I'm so excited about what I've seen here so far that I'm completely laid back and comfortable in my approach. I'm answering all his questions as if I already have the job and we're just going through the motions right now. He tries to keep the interview professional, but I soon find out that he's married. He married the girl of his dreams two years out of college. He is in his early thirties and he has three kids, all hers from a previous marriage. I also find out that she's six years older than he is and apparently super-hot. He keeps saying that he can't bring her to the holiday parties because all the young guys in the office keep trying to hit on her. We hit it off so well that he begins to give me the lowdown.

Brad explains, "Listen, here is what we would generally do at this point. I would send you home and give my recommendations to the manager in the department that I believe you would be a good fit in. Then, he would have you come back and interview with him. If he liked you, you would then be asked to come back for one final time and interview with our GM. Instead of wasting your time and ours, I'm going to recommend that you see all three of us today."

I'm shocked, "Wow. Thanks!"

Brad asks, "How much time do you have?"

I say, "I have all day!"

Oh, I immediately wish I could take that last sentence back. I don't want to give the impression that I am desperate for a well-paying job, even though I am. Plus, I have another interview to get to and I have Eric in his car downstairs waiting for me.

Brad smiles. "Great! Let me get with the other guys and I'll send them in when they're ready!"

Brad gets up and immediately leaves the room. As soon as he does I grab my cell phone to check the time and it's 10:30!

Wow, I've been here over an hour already. I've got my next interview lined up for 12:30. I really hope this doesn't take long. Every second passed like minutes, and every minute passes like hours. I think that every person that comes even inches away from the glass door of my interview room is the next person to interviewing me. Remember, I have no idea who they are or what they look like. But no, for the most part, male or female, they come by the conference room to peek inside and continue walking. Every single one of them stares at me like I'm exotic zoo animal placed in a glass cage. It's kind of getting annoying. I look down at my phone again, 10:45 a.m. Just as I'm about to look up from my phone again, the door opens.

A man I've never seen before says, "Hi! My name is Donald. You can call me Don."
I smile, "Like Don Juan?"
He chuckles. "I haven't been Don Juan in quite some time!" He points to his beer belly and rubs it.

Don is clean shaven. He's is in his late thirties and is much taller and heavier than Brad. My first thought when I saw Don was, *What the heck are they feeding you guys here?* Don is a big guy and barely fits in the over-sized chairs in this room, but he makes it work. He sits down, and I can see that he has my resume in his hands. As he starts to go over it, I speak first. I don't want to give him the opportunity to run this interview and I want to pick up in this interview right where I left off with Brad. I start conversation and small talk.

I say, "Oh, I see you're married too, just like Brad."
Don nods. "Yeah, ten years and two beautiful kids…plus a dog."
"And what? No white picket fences?"
He jokes, "We had one, but the dog ate it."
"Good one sir!"
We both laugh.
I ask, "So what is it that you do here?"
Don explains, "Well, I run the new business sign-up departments, and if you were hired, you would be working for me in my group."
"And what is it that your group does?"
"We make it easy for new business owners to set up LLC's or corporations here in Nevada. We handle all aspects setting the entity up and taking care of all the paperwork. We do all the filings for them and in exchange they pay us a fee," Don says.
I nod, "Very cool."

He continues, "Three quarters of your day would be on the phones with new business owners. The remaining twenty-five percent of the time you will be responding to emails, or following up on new business filings that you filed through the state for our customers."

I keep control of the conversation by asking all the questions and allowing him to give me all the answers. We also get personal again. He tells me that he also grew up in Jersey and that he was born in Cape May. In my mind, he might as well have been born in Delaware, but I hold that in. We laugh for a bit and begin to crack jokes about the difference between the people who live in South Jersey (Eagles football team fans) and the people who live in North Jersey (NY Giants fans). The only thing that breaks up our shit-talking laugh fest is the fact that he looks down at his watch and realized that we were speaking for close to thirty-five minutes. He immediately puts his work face back on.

Don says, "Okay, Holis. Obviously, I like you. I'm going to forward my recommendations to our GM and have him come speak with you as soon as he's ready. Can you stick around?"
I'm exuberant. "Fantastic! Yes of course."
"Great! I'll send him in," Don says. "Good luck to ya. Nice to meet you!"

Just like that, Don leaves the room and I just knocked interview number two out for the count. I'm one step away and one interview away from getting this job, I just know it! I use the time alone to grab my phone and check the time.

11:05 a.m. We're cutting it close, I must be at my next interview at 12:30. I hope I get this job, because if I don't and I run late for my next interview, I'm going to be screwed. I take the time to shoot Eric a quick text to update him on my status. *I'm on interview number 3!* I also make sure he's alright and still here. He sends me a text back to let me know that he's fine and that he's in the car napping. Good, because even if I don't make it to my next company that I'm interviewing with, at least I still have a ride home. I put my phone back in my pocket and begin to tap my fingers on this executive size table that could fit sixteen. Even with the over-sized leather chairs, I find myself again counting away the minutes trying to figure out when the GM is finally going to make his appearance.

11:15 a.m. passes.
11:25 a.m. passes.
Okay, if this guy isn't here in the next five minutes, I'm going. The next company that I need to interview with today is at 12:30 and is about a half hour away, without traffic, and I want to be there early to make a good impression. 11:27... 11:29... 11:35 – That's it, I'm out of here! I get up to leave the room to find Brad to let him know that I can't stay any longer, that we will have to reschedule my last interview with the GM for another day. As soon

as I get up, boom! The door opens and it's the GM. Before I know it, he's in the room and in his interview chair in 3.5 milliseconds. I'm still caught in a moment and in awe with how fast it took for the GM to barge in here and get to his chair…that I just start stretching!

"Sorry, you caught me stretching, been here since 9:15. I didn't want my legs to fall asleep on me," I say jokingly with a smile on my face. I can't help it. I don't know if he can tell, but it was my first reaction to try to cover up the fact that he might have just caught me trying to leave.

Nothing from the GM. He's dead silent and he points to the chair where I was just sitting to motion that I should have a seat. Embarrassed, I immediately do so. He has my resume in his hands as he looks down on it. He skims over page number one, then page number two. I try again to pick up right where I left off with Don. I use this quiet time to open to small talk and conversations but most importantly, so that I can get control of the situation back. I ask:

I say, "So you must be the GM!"
The GM is silent.
"Done any good stretching lately?" I say jokingly, of course.
The GM is still silent.

Nothing from this guy. I quickly look him over to see if I can find something to talk about and get this guy to open up. I look at his fingers and don't see a wedding ring. I look at his watch and I can't tell what kind it is from here. I try to lean back in my chair so that I could get a glance under the table and check out his shoes, praying that maybe I used to own the same ones before I went homeless. Just as I got back far enough…he looks up from my resume and speaks.

"Tell me about a time when you wanted to physically hurt your boss but didn't and how you overcame it?"

I'm stunned, to say the least. I'm sorry, what?"

He asks again, "Tell me about a time when you wanted to physically hurt your boss but didn't, and what was the outcome?"

What kind of question is that to start off an interview with? I sit up in my chair and I try to answer back the best way that I could while being politically correct at the same time. "Well, I would never want to hurt my boss, but if the time did come I would…"

He cuts me off.

"Tell me about a time when you wanted to go off on a customer but couldn't, and how you calmed yourself down from doing so?"
Again, here I am trying to be as politically correct as possible. "I would never want to curse out or go off on a customer but, if the time did ever come…"
He cuts me off again. This guy won't let me get one-word in. He asks, "If you could punch one person in the face, who would it be and why?"

I have a mental image of myself right now throwing my hands up and asking this guy, *are you crazy or something, what kind of questions are these?* This time I try not to stay politically correct since the first two answers obviously didn't work for him. I say, "I tell you what, you know who I would love to punch in the face…"

As soon as I say the word "face", he's up and gone. He lets out a quick "thank you" and is out of the conference room just as fast as he came in. It takes about five seconds for my brain to catch up to what just happened and for me give up, throw my hands up. I finally let out a *what the fuck just happened?*

In no less than thirty seconds Brad opens the door to the conference room.

Brad asks me, "So, how did it go?"
I'm still puzzled. "I uh, I um…"
Brad lets out a little smile. "It's all right. Come with me."

I get up and we make our way back past the sales floor. At first, I'm thinking that maybe it was an inside joke. That maybe they do this as an initiation to all the new hires. That maybe the only real person that I had to get through was Don.

Just as we're about to walk past the receptionist desk I'm thinking, *maybe we're headed the new employee training room where I can fill out new employee forms.* Brad holds, points to his left, and notions me out to the lobby. I'm in front of him at this moment and I can hear that he's stopped walking, so I turn around. Brad has his hand out as if he was looking for a handshake. I oblige.

Brad declares, "I'm sorry, but it looks like you're not a good fit for what we are looking for. Have a good day, and good luck to ya."

Brad turns and walks away. I'm still in shock. I look over at the receptionist to get sign that they are kidding with me. She doesn't dare to look in my direction. *Just part of her job,* I'm sure she tells herself. After what feels like forever, I finally realize that it's not a joke. That Brad is not coming back for me and that I should probably make my way back to the elevator now before I really make an ass out of myself.

I make my way to the elevator and push the button for the elevator to take me back downstairs. The elevator door opens, and I get in. I'm still trying to process what happened… I seriously thought I had this one.
I get downstairs and walk through the lobby and out the building. I find Eric's car and it looks like he's awake now. He's in the driver seat looking down, which means he's probably playing on his phone. I get to his car and knock on the passenger side window, he unlocks the doors. I get in.

Eric says jokingly, "Almost over two and a half hours. I hope you at least got a blow job while you were up there!"
I say nothing. He can tell that the interview didn't go as well as planned.

Eric asks, "What happened?"
I sigh. "Nothing. I didn't get the job. Did you say almost two and a half hours?"
Eric nods, "Yeah, you were gone a long time."
I grab my phone out of my pocket to check the time. It's 11:45.
"Bro, you need to book it," I say. "I still have time to get to my next interview on time!"
Eric starts the car. "Do we have an address?"
I tap my phone. "I'm on it. One second."

I open the maps on my phone and enter the address for my next interview in it. We can't waste any time trying to get there using back roads.

I exclaim, "Got it! Let's go!"

And Eric takes off as if he's going to win a medal for best time when we get there. He's driving like we're firefighters on our way to put out a burning building with children in it. We head up Sahara going west. We cross over Durango and hit Fort Apache. We're now in Summerlin, one of the nicer parts of town. I know this place well because I've lived in this part of town for years, right before I lost everything, so I have a pretty good idea of where we are at. We take a left onto Fort Apache and get down to Hualapai. We take a left, a few rights and then enter a... housing community? I look down at my navigation app on my phone, puzzled. I look up again and before I know it, my navigation app lets out a *you have arrived at your destination* alert. I look left, I look right, I look at Eric and he's just as puzzled.

Eric asks, "Is this it?"
"It can't be," I say. "I don't see any buildings or corporate offices."

I exit out of the navigation app to call the company that I'm supposed to interview for next. Now that we're officially lost, I'm going to be officially late. I dial their phone number and a man picks up. We'll call him Jerry.

Jerry answers, "Hello! Thanks for calling. This is Jerry, how may I assist you?"
I say, "Yeah, hi Jerry. My name is Holis. I have an interview with you at 12:30 and it looks like I'm going to be late. The address that I wrote down for you guys took me to a house."
Jerry asks, "Are you at that house now?"
"Yes."
There's a pause.
He says, "Then you're not going to be late. You're actually right on time because that house is actually us!"
"It is?"
Jerry insists, "Yep, it sure is! Come on up when you're ready!"
He hangs up, and again for the second time in less than an hour today, I find myself completely confused.
Eric then breaks my confusion with a question. "Well, what's going on?"
"I have no idea. He said that this is them."

Eric points to it. "You mean this house right here?

"Yeah."
Eric prods, "Well? Are you going in there or what?"

I'm aghast. "Are you kidding me? I'm not going in there. This is obviously a fly-by-night company, and that's if they're even a legit one at that. I just got fucked over by a company like this, plus it's in some dude's house. He could be a serial killer for all I know. I could go in there and get chopped up into a million pieces and fed to local pigeons in the park by midnight tonight. No, I'm not going in there. This has 'sketchy' written all over it and he's not going to be able to pay me what I'm looking for anyways."

Eric says, "Man, after everything that you've been through, you better go up there and interview for this job. You've slept in public bathrooms. You've eaten out of dumpsters and garbage cans. You've counted loose change found in the cracks of sidewalks to be able to afford something to eat that wasn't covered in ants. You've slept on the ground and made me take four hours out of my day to move people of Craigslist for fifty bucks. You better go up there and not only interview this job but get this job right now!"

Eric unlocks his doors. He leans over and opens mine. Nothing is said, and I feel like I just got told off by my grandfather. Not that Eric is that old, but my Grandfather was usually the only person who would talk to me that way. I'm hesitant but I eventually get out, not without having the last word though, "Fine, but if I get cut up into a million pieces and fed to pigeons, I'm gonna be pissed at you."

He waves his hand at me saying, "Go! You got this!"
I close the passenger door behind me and make my way up the sidewalk to this dude's house. I reach the front door and ring the doorbell. After a minute or two, the door answers and this clean-shaven man, no more than five feet eight inches tall, frail, in his forties, with a short, and trimmed hair cut answers the door.

"You must be Holis. I'm Jerry, come on in."

We shake hands and even his handshake is weak. He has a deep baritone voice for someone so frail and he's polite, even though he's very straight to the point. I would not be surprised if he had military in his background. Not him personally, not by his handshake, but possibly someone in his immediate family has served. My first thought is, *well, if he tries to chop me up in a million pieces at least I'll have a fighting chance before he does.*

He closes the door behind me and says, "Follow me." I immediately notice the sunken-in living room, the family room and can see the kitchen from where I am at. It's an open floor plan and looks exactly like what I would imagine it to look like. Somebody's house. His house, I'm assuming, was built about a decade ago and by the looks of things, that was probably the last time they bought furniture for this place too. He says, "This way."

I begin to follow him as he makes his way up the stairs to the second floor. I can't help but think, *Only I can go on two interviews back to back where one of them is in a fifteen-story building with glass and marble everywhere, and the other is in some dude's house. What the heck is going on here?*

We go up to the second floor and we immediately come to a loft. Now, usually in this area you would find toys where the kids could play or if you were single this would be your man cave area. Not with this guy. He turned this entire loft area into a makeshift sales floor, complete with two cubicles, a huge black and white dry erase board. There's scribble on it, and a wooden table in the center of the room with chairs for impromptu meetings.

Speaking of meetings, it looks like I'm about to join one. It also looks like this won't be a one-on-one interview, but an interview with four other people as well. I know this because these people all seem to have my resume laid flat in front of them on the table. *Firing squad type of interview, I guess. Just don't ask me to join your cult.* They have their backs to me as I make my way into the loft area, so I have to walk around to the opposite side of the table to be able to sit down.

As I make my way I notice an older woman who's in her late forties with long dirty blonde hair, physically fit, the first three buttons on her power suit are unbuttoned and she's not afraid to show her exceptional qualities (if you know what I mean.) I try my absolute best not to stare at her. Obviously, she must be Jerry's wife or girlfriend because she's sitting next to the head of the table, so before Jerry even has a chance to sit down, I already know exactly where he'll be sitting. The others at the table are much younger males and look very tech savvy. I'm can only assume that one is a programmer and the other one is a designer.

Jerry and I both take a seat at the table at the same time. He introduces everyone sitting there. Amalia, who he introduces as the V.P. (his girlfriend), David, who he introduces as the programmer and Vic, who he introduces as the designer (damn, I'm good). He finally introduces himself as the president and owner of their little mobile app company.

I'm still in shock that I didn't get the job at the last interview that I was at, in a building fifteen stories tall made with all marble and glass and with luxury decor in the lobby. I would have been proud to say that I worked there.

Here, on the other hand, I'm not excited about. I'm just going through the motions because I don't think Eric would have let us leave without me at least coming in here and giving this place a shot, even if it meant working out of some dude's house. Jerry, again being friendly but straightforward, dives right into the interview.

Jerry asks, "So, have you ever sold mobile apps before?"
I shake my head, "No."
"Are you familiar with mobile apps, specifically mobile apps that are designed for businesses?"
I reply, "Not really."

Jerry asks, "Have you gone to our website to see what we are all about and what we build for businesses via mobile apps?"
I answer, "No. I didn't have the time to."
You can tell that I'm not too excited about this interview.
Jerry says, "Here, let me show you."
David quips, "Well, at least he's honest."

Jerry proceeds to pull out an iPad from one of his sleeves and types something into the web browser. As soon as he finds what he's looking for, he slides it across the table in my direction. I pick up the iPad and start to look at what they do. Impressive for the most part, but I'm still not sold, and my hands aren't clammy at this point. I'm waiting for the punch line.

The *"We are a startup and can't afford you, so this job will be commission only for the right individual"* or *"We pay a draw vs. commission here where you will have to pay for your seat, phone and computer once you commission out."* Like my old job did to me. That's what I'm waiting for. Jerry squeezes out a few more interviewing questions.

Jerry explains, "Holis, what we do is build and create custom apps for small business owners. We not only create custom apps, but we also launch them in iTunes and the Google Play store for our customers. We give them 24/7 support and offer back-end SEO for their apps so that they can easily be found in the iTunes and Google Play store.
Do you think you could sell what we do for small business owners?"

After a little thought, I reply, "Well, I tell you what. I can see how this is a necessity for small business owners and not just a benefit. With mobile phones outpacing desktop computers, laptops, and even tablets today, how could you *not* have a mobile app for your business? Especially if you own a service business that is B2C (business to customer.)"

Jerry says, "Well, I think that's it. Does anyone have any questions for Holis?"

Not one word is said. Everyone is dead silent. I can't tell if I said the right thing or the wrong thing.

Jerry concludes, "Okay, Holis, well then, I'll walk you out."

Once again, I am completely confused. I thought this was going to be an all-out war with questions from all angles about my sales ability. Where I've worked before and if I have references. The only person asking the questions was Jerry and we didn't talk about any of those topics. Why was everyone else at the table for? Intimidation?

We get downstairs and I've had enough of not knowing and being confused for one day. As he opens the door to let me out, I had to ask.

"So, did I get the job or not?"

Jerry says, "We'll call you."

He rushes me out the door, and the door slams behind me. I look down at my feet and then look over at Eric in the car. He shrugs his shoulders as if to say, *oh well, at least you gave it your best shot.* I shrugged back as to say *oh well, at least I'm not dead.* I make my way back to his car, I hop in and we make our way out of the community.

Eric asks, "Where to now?"

I sigh, "Home. I think I've had enough with being confused and disappointment for one day."

CHAPTER TWENTY-FOUR
I just need an opportunity

CHAPTER TWENTY-FOUR
I just need an opportunity

WELL, I WOKE UP TO THE FACT THAT TODAY IS CHRISTMAS. I've been searching non-stop, day in and day out for a job. Maybe it's that time of year where companies aren't hiring, but I feel as if I've submitted at least three hundred resumes to open positions online, and yet not one person has called me back. I haven't received many inquiries from my Craigslist ads to help move people either. To say the least, it's been tough. I'm completely embarrassed in myself because I haven't made one dollar to be able to buy my son a gift for Christmas. What kind of father am I? Also, for the first time in a long time I haven't made it back to Jersey to celebrate the holidays with my family.

It's true what they say about the holidays, they do become lonely. The depression starts to set in. I've thought about killing myself twice now in the past seven months. Both times I was sad, lonely and depressed. I had felt like the weight of the world was on my shoulders and with every day that passed that weight only became heavier. I also thought that the world would be a better place without me in it, but this time instead of contemplating killing myself on the bathroom floor in a public restroom, I'm thinking about it on the floor in my bedroom in my own house. Funny how those feelings, if you let them in, will follow you anywhere, no matter if you're living in a cardboard box or in a ten-room mansion.

Before I can give it another thought, my phone rings. I'm not expecting any calls but then again, it is Christmas and my family from back East might be calling to wish me a happy holiday.

I find my phone under my bed on the third ring. I look down to check the caller I.D. and it's my ex. *Great, she's probably calling me to remind me of how much of an awful dad I am because I couldn't buy him one gift.* I take a deep breath to prepare myself and then hit the answer key.

"Hello."
She says, "Merry Christmas!"
"Thanks."
"What's wrong?" she asks.
"Nothing." I switch the conversation because I don't feel like talking about what I was thinking about prior to her call. "Is lil' man up yet?"
"He is."
I explain, "I'm sorry that I could not buy him a gift. The past couple of weeks have been hard really and I haven't found a job yet. I also haven't been called for any new job interviews since the last two that I went on."

"Where are you? Are you in Jersey?" she asks.
"No. I'm home. I am in Vegas."
She inquires, "How come you didn't celebrate Christmas at your girlfriend's house?"
"You know that's the farthest thing on my mind right now, having a girlfriend, right?" I huff.
There's a bit of silence between us.
She says, "I guess. Well, we were about to open up presents but I'll make him wait if you can find a way down here?"
I'm quiet for a moment, completely stunned.
She says, "Hello?"

I stammer, "Yes, I'm here. Are you saying that I can join him for Christmas?"
"Yeah, I mean it is Christmas and you shouldn't be by yourself" she says.
I try hard to fight it, but I can't stop from a single tear from finding its way down my cheek.
I ask, "Do you mind if I get your address from you?"
She replies, "No that's fine. It's 1749 D…R Street. Unit B."
I can't believe she just gave me her address.
"I'll be there in 20 minutes," I assure her. "Oh…and thank you."
"You're welcome. See you in a bit."

We hang up.

Somebody in the clouds above must still love me because I was just seconds from falling back into depression again and she calls. Not only does she call, but she also gives me her address. She's never given me her address before. I must admit, I feel absolutely better now. She's never asked me to come over to her house…ever. We've always met at public places and halfway points for me to see him. How is this possible? Why is she being so nice? Never mind that. We have a mission to accomplish: to get down to her house so that I can see my boy on Christmas day! Oh, and dear Universe, thank you for that call. Who knows what I would have done if I would have continued thinking the way I was thinking before she had called.
You do have great timing. So again, thank you.

I consider my secret stash to see how much cash I have on me, which by the way, isn't so secret, it's an envelope that I keep cash in underneath my pillow. Five bucks. Story of my life. I do not have enough money for a rideshare and I'm not calling Eric, he's done so much for me already, and I know for a fact that he is at his uncle's house celebrating Christmas. There's no way I'm going to bother him for a ride today. The only hope that I have is my roommate. I know he's home today because he mentioned that he wasn't going to be celebrating Christmas with his family this year. My only hope is that he's up and that he won't mind giving me a ride. I get up and peek out my door to see if he is sitting in the living room or if in the kitchen. Nothing, it's as silent as night. I open my door completely and look down to see if his bedroom door is open. Nope, dead end there too. His door is closed. I close my door and start to think. *How do I ask him if he's awake and if he can give me a ride without knocking on his door or bothering him?*

Oh, I got it! I send him a text asking him if he's awake.
I get a text back with, "Yeah, what's up?"
My reply, "Merry Christmas, bro. I have a favor to ask of you."
"Merry Christmas back. Sure, what is it?"
I type in, "I need a ride to go see my boy. My ex invited me over to see him for Christmas."
"No shit."
"Yeah, exactly. Could you hook me up with a ride to go see him?"
Ben says, "Absolutely. Shoot me the address. I'll be ready in fifteen."

I shoot him the address via text. Oh man, this is so awesome. I'm about to see lil' man for Christmas. I look around to see what I can bring with me to give him as a present. My old desktop computer for Eric's old office? No. My bed? Obviously not. I have nothing to give him, but hopefully me being there is just enough.

At the speed of light, I'm dressed and just as I'm putting on my shoes I hear my roommate's door open, so I know he's ready. I open my bedroom door just as he's passing my door on his way to the kitchen for something to drink.
Ben asks, "You ready?"
"Yeah."
"Okay," he says. "Let me grab bottled water and we can go."
"Cool. Hey, do you think that you can give me a ride back, too?"
Ben nods. "Yeah, I had no plans to do anything today anyways."

"Awesome, I really appreciate it," I say. "Thanks again."
He grabs his bottled water and we head out. As we lock up the door to our apartment and head down the stairs, he mentions, "I don't know if you know, but your ex's place is literally ten minutes from here, so it's not far at all." I'm a little surprised. "No, I didn't check. With being so excited I forgot to look up her address."

We head out to his car, get in and we're officially off. I couldn't tell you about the car ride or how many turns we've made because the entire time, I was playing out in my head how this was going to go when I see him…when I see her. I can already picture her slamming the door in my face when she realizes that I showed up without any presents in my hands for him. I picture myself having to text Ben back asking him to turn around and come pick me up because she changed her mind about me seeing my son. The worst kinds of scenarios are going through my head and I can't help it. We had the kind of relationship where that kind of behavior from her would be justified.

Before I know it, he takes a left into a ten-year-old townhouse community, his car comes to a slow crawl as he pulls over to the right and mentions, "We're here."
My immediate thought is, *so this is where you moved to the day we got evicted out of our condo. Nice place.*

I also noticed that Ben pulled over right in front of her building and that I can see Townhouse Unit B from where we are parked. It's just a matter of fifteen feet or so. I shake his hand and open my door to get out. I close the passenger door behind me and make my way to her door.

It's a cool day in December for Vegas. I'm in a light sweater, and there are leaves on the ground where she lives. I remember the crispness of the air with every breath and every step I took. I get to her door and ring the doorbell.

Here goes nothing...

If she slams the door in my face, she better do it now while Ben is still in the parking lot. The door opens and it's her. She looks good, in her tiny little Mexican self. There is a moment of silence and one last breath of crisp air before she says, "Hi."
"Hey," I respond.

She hasn't slammed the door in my face yet. This must be a good thing.
She says, "Well, come on in."

I look back to see if Ben is still here just in case she throws me out seconds after entering. I don't even notice or hear his car leave, but he did. He's gone. I guess I'm committed at this point. I make my way inside. There is a Christmas tree to my immediate right that is filled with presents from the floor up to the bottom of the tree. The tree is nicely decorated as well. I can't help but ask myself, *where did she get the money to buy so many gifts?* Within the first three steps I've already scanned the entire downstairs.

Unlike her, I've always been conscious of my surroundings. Everything here seems to be second-hand except for the dining room table, which was brand new. The TV stand that is holding up the flat screen TV I bought her two Christmas's ago, the last one we spent together as a family, looks to be brand new as well. She must have gone back to storage afterwards and pulled it out of there. I remember Eric and I packed that flat screen in the storage the night before the constable showed up to throw us out of our place. The couch is second-hand, but in good shape except for the stains here and there which were obviously caused by lil' man. Speaking of, I ask, "How are you?" She shrugs, "I'm good."
"Where is he?"
She says, "He's upstairs playing. I'll call him down."
She closes the door behind me and yells, "Daddy's here!"

I look back at her and she gives me a courtesy smile back to say, *Yes, I just did call you daddy.* It's a polite exchange and there seems to be an understanding in the air that today of all days, we will not be fighting. That she seems to have no intentions of picking a fight with me because today is Christmas, and today it's all about my lil' man.

I look again towards the stairs because I hear his voice getting louder as he seems to exit a room upstairs and making his way towards the stairs to come down. He finally arrives to the top of the stairs. He looks amazing! He rushes to the stairs and before I can react, he's already making his way down the stairs, one step at a time. While grasping onto the railing he steps down one step, one step, he keeps stepping down until he's at the bottom of the stairs. I look back at my ex and say, "Are you kidding me? He's walking down the steps now? The last time I saw him in a home around steps he was trying to crawl up them!"

She replies, "Yep, and he's fast too, really fast!"
He makes a beeline for his mom, almost as if I wasn't even standing here. It's okay. I'm still in awe that he can make it down the steps by himself.

He holds a small toy truck that fits in the palm of his left hand up in the air almost as to say, "Look Mom, look what I've found." She replies back to him, as if she knew what he said and says "I know, look who's here! Daddy's here!" She grabs him by the same hand that the toy truck is in and walks him over to me. I bend down on both knees so that I can meet him at eye level and say, "What are you doing? What is that in your hands?"

With his right hand, he points to the truck in his left and mumbles something that resembles, "It's my truck!" My heart melts. He doesn't know how to speak yet, but he's very smart. You can tell by the way he pauses in between each thought he tries to relay, and how he uses his pointer finger to bring attention to what he's talking about. He might not have the words to match his action yet, but I can tell that he's having a full conversation with me in his head right now.

I pick him up and give him the biggest hug ever, as I carry him over to their second-hand couch to sit down with him. Just as I sit down and place him in my lap, I can see that my ex had made it over to the tree and she's starting to pull gifts out from underneath.

My ex asks him, "Which presents do you want to open up first? This one is from Grandpa!" as she pulls one single gift out from underneath the tree. "And this one is from Grandma!" She pulls another gift out from underneath the tree. "And this one is from Momma!" A much bigger gift that is obviously a gift wrapped small soccer ball. "And…" She pauses, and I see her pull another gift out from underneath the tree. She immediately pulls the label off and crumbles it, throwing it behind her, and says "And this one is from Daddy!"

Realizing what she had just done, deep down inside, I cry. I mean I start to cry from deep down inside my stomach on up. She could tell as it's even hard to stop my eyes from watering up. She gives me a nod and smiles as she hands me the gift that was previously from someone else to give to him. She does this a few times and I know the gifts that she's ripping labels off and throwing them behind her back are originally from her. One of many gifts that she had bought him for Christmas, but she didn't have to do that. She didn't have to sacrifice one of her own gifts to him just to include me in the moment. She didn't, but she did.

It's funny. At this exact moment, you could have lined me up in front of three hundred of the closest people that I knew before I lost it all, on the busiest

intersection on Las Vegas Boulevard, and all of them would have walked up to me and said things like, "What happened to you?"
"Have you seen yourself lately?"
"How could you have let this happen to yourself?"
"We're no longer friends because you eat your dinner out of a garbage can."

I tell you, I still would not have felt any bigger of a piece of shit than how I do right now. At my ex's house on Christmas day, no money, no job, bummed a ride to get here and came without a single present for my son.

I also know that in this same exact moment that because of her actions, that I will always have her back. I also know that we will never again be together as a family, and I get that. At this moment, I'd rather never be with her again, keep her in my life as my son's mom, than to be with her, for a moment in time, and lose her forever again. There is no better mom for him when it comes to her. For that, she will always have my eternal love and respect. I know that she will move on and meet someone who will give her that which I could not, love, respect, and marriage. If whoever she meets will treat my son with the same matter of respect that I treat her, then I will wish for them both a great life together.

I also know that I will meet someone new who I will love unconditionally too, but that person must know, that there will always be a place in my heart that is reserved for my son's mom. The same way you will love your mother like none other, or your brother like none other, your sister, your father, like none other, I will love her like none other. I will love her as my son's mom, the same way, always.

We spend the rest of the morning opening gifts and watching him rip through them like a tidal wave. We spend the day together, not like a family, but like friends that will know each other forever. My son on the other hand... well of course, he's my Mini-Me. I'll always have his back too. I am eternally grateful for this day that we shared, and I will never forget it. To say to myself that I'd gone full circle, from having it all to losing it, to getting back on my feet again, it would have been a lie. I only now know that my new life will never come full circle, it will only get better.

Thinking about it now, I can tell you that I am more grateful today with the life that I have than I've ever been. I only have a sliver of what I had when I thought I was successful and, yet I am still more grateful today with less than I have ever been. I can tell you honestly that even before my fall when I had all the things that society says you need to be successful, that I was never happy.

There was always a huge hole in the center of my core that I could not fill up, no matter what I had or tried to fill it with. Today I know that I am whole. Those thoughts that I was having about suicide when I was homeless and right before she called, I'm never having those thoughts ever again. That's a promise. Can you imagine if I would have acted on just one of those thoughts and succeeded? I'll tell you what, for starters, you wouldn't be reading this book right now. This book wouldn't even exist.

So yeah, I don't have friends with impressive 'Titles' anymore. I don't drive high end cars anymore....Heck, I don't even have a car. What I do have is love and a whole lot of it. I have a love for life. I'm learning to love my experience and what I've gone through. I love my son and I love having him back in my life. I have the best relationship I could ever ask for with his mom. I love the fact that I'm humble now. That I have gratitude. For the first time ever, I have me. Complete.

The day turns into evening and I must be going. I call my roommate to see if he can come and get me. He mentions that he's on his way. With time to spare, I take a very tired my lil' man upstairs to his room to sleep. He fell asleep on the couch about an hour ago, but I think he would rather wake up in his own bed than on the couch in the living room, so I very carefully and quietly carry him up the stairs and to his bedroom. I lay him in his bed so very softly and pull the cover up over him so that he can rest comfortably.

I make my way downstairs to start saying goodbye, and to let her know I appreciate everything that she did today. That I forgive her for leaving me on the day we got evicted from our unit. I know now that it was something that I had to go through to prepare me for whatever it is that comes next. I know that she had no choice in the matter, it was written to happen exactly the way it did. She obviously has no idea what I'm talking about, but shakes her head in agreement and says, "Thank you." She's never believed in the power of the universe. She's always had a scientific and analytic mind, which is why being a paralegal is the perfect job for her until she becomes a successful lawyer one day.

I get a text from Brad. He's here. We hug and we both give our final goodbyes for the day and I take off.

The next day I wake with more energy than ever. I wake up at four a.m. and I'm out of my house by 4:30 to go on my walk. I've began to use this time to speak to the universe and to speak positive affirmations and gratefulness into my life. It's become something of a ritual, but I don't mind, it seems like the right thing to do and for some reason, it's starting to become much more natural to do also. I get back home and jump into my regular routine. A hundred and twenty push-ups, a shower, and then eat. I do my normal push-ups and run off to take a shower. I get out and make my way back to my room and as soon as I close the door I hear a notification

go off on my phone, the one that lets me know that I've missed a call. The only person that would call me this early is my Mom. I've been on the West Coast now for close to nine years now and every time my mom calls, she calls me at Six a.m. She always starts off by saying that it's 9 am on the East Coast, she always apologizes, and proceeds to keep talking. I've gotten used to the fact that when she calls, and I answer, that I can forget about going back to sleep. I walk over to my bed to turn my phone over and see who called. I bet it was her. She probably wants to know if I got to see my boy yesterday for the holiday and when she can expect pictures. I flip my phone over and it's… a California number?

Who's calling me at this early in the morning from California? I don't know anyone in California? Obviously, a telemarketer, and you know what?

I'm going to call them back and let them know that this is my cell phone. That I don't appreciate telemarketing calls to my cell phone at seven a.m. and how I can't wait to give them a piece of my mind. As I stand in the center of my bedroom, naked with a towel around my waist, I open my phone and press redial. The phone rings and then there's an answer.

The voice on the other line answers, "Hello?"

I say, "Yes, I'm calling you back. I saw that I had missed your call."
The voice on the other line sounds confused. "And who is this?"
With attitude, I reply, "This is Holis. Who is this?"

The voice on the other line, much more pleasant now, says, "Oh! Holis! Yes, how are you? This is Jerry. I don't know if you remember, but you came down and interviewed with us a few weeks ago for a job position we had open. You had interviewed for the sales position for our mobile app startup company."

Um, it's seven a.m. the day after Christmas, why is this dude is calling me? He better not be calling me this early the day after Christmas to tell me that they 'Decided to go in another direction.'

I reply, "Yes, I remember. How can I help you?"

Jerry says, "Well, we've been talking about you since the day you left. My Vice President and I were just looking over your resume and I have to say, we were really impressed with you." "Well, thank you." He still hasn't said why he was calling.
Jerry says, "I apologize for calling you this early the day after Christmas. We start here at 6 a.m., and even though the company is closed now for the holidays, some habits are hard to break, I guess. So, I was wondering if you found a job yet."

"No, not yet. It's Christmas I guess."

Jerry says with a bit of a sigh, "Well, I'm afraid that I have some good news and some bad news for you. The bad news is, the company, like you said, is closed now for the holiday break. We will not open until January Fifth of next year. The good news is that we would like to hire you!"

I drop my towel in shock, just complete surprise. I'm now standing in the center of my room totally naked. By the way, my windows do not have any window coverings or shades.

The conversation continues:
I ask, "Really?"
Jerry says, "Yes."

"I don't know what to say...but thank you!"
"You're welcome," Jerry chuckles.

"Wow. That's so awesome. You have no idea how much this means to me."
Jerry says, "And Holis?"
"Yes!"
Jerry explains, "The position pays seven-hundred a week. I hope you're fine with that."
I'm silent for some forty seconds as I glance over at my last five dollars in my white envelope that sitting under my pillow right now.
Jerry asks, "Holis?"
I stammer, "I'm sorry, can you repeat that again?"
"The position pays seven hundred dollars a week. Twenty-eight hundred a month base with 20% commissions. Are you okay with that?"
I exclaim, "Abso-fucking-lutely!"
"Excuse me?"

I say, "I'm sorry, I mean yes! I'm just so excited to get started!"

Jerry continues, "Well, like I said, we're closed right now for the holidays and don't open back up until January Fifth. So, I guess the only question is...can you be here for your first day on January Fifth?"

I mentally pee myself and start to cry tears of joy. I can't believe he hired me, I can't believe that I'm about to go from Zero to $2,800 a month! I can't help, but feel like I've just been born again. That this is my opportunity to officially get back on my feet and kick some ass and you better believe that I am not going to waste no one moment of this.

I finally reply back
"I can start whenever you want me to. I've been prepared and ready for an opportunity just like this."

He says "Great! I'll see you here on January Fifth at 6 am." "And Holis..."
"Yes" I reply
"Be sure to bring your A game."
Oh he has no idea...

All I needed was an opportunity and now I truly have one.
This is going to be the start to a brand new me...I can feel it.
All I needed to do was believe.
Believe that I was better.
Better than my circumstances.
Better than my situation.
Better than the garbage can I was eating out of...
Better than this.
Now that I'm feeling better about myself, how about I get dressed before I start to scare my neighbors? Fuck it...Not before I first bust out in my happy dance.

You don't want to see this. It's not a pretty sight.

Thank you once again Eric for motivating me to go into that 'Sketchy house' and who would have thought that, that 'Sketchy interview' in that 'Sketchy house' would have been the launching pad for my new lease on life.

Looking at what I had gone through up to this point; I have a house, I have a roof over my head, I have security, I have a bed, I've met some really cool people, I've met some really bad people, I've been tempted, I picked up a great friend in Eric, I have my son back in my life, I have a little bit of food in my refrigerator, I have my confidence, I've overcame obstacles, I've gained a positive mind, and I now have a job that's paying me five times more than the job that I had before going homeless.

I say in complete gratitude, "I wonder where this journey will take me next?" Where ever it is, I hope that it feels a lot like this. That it feels like...Home.

BETTER THAN THIS

Bonus chapter

MY SEVEN STEPS.

Seven Steps to Getting Out of Your Situation Fast

ONE OF THE QUESTIONS I GET ASKED ALL THE TIME IS "How did I do it?" "Once you got back on your feet, how did you go from homelessness to hopeful and change your entire world in just a few short years?" My answer is always the same; "With a lot of help, hard work, hard days, and Seven ways." These Seven ways have been a game-changer for me, my life, and I still use them today. These Seven steps are the ones that I took to go from squatting in abandoned offices and eating out of garbage cans to destroying my battle with depression and winning.

With these exact seven steps, I believe, that if you follow them exactly in the same order in which I walked them in, that you too will find hope and get out of your situation. Any situation, fast. Whether you're not happy in your current job, or you're not happy in your relationship, or if you feel as if you're just existing and not living out your true purpose...just know that if you follow these Seven steps exactly, that you too can change your life for the better. Quickly. Remember, you must be willing to do the 'work' to get there. So, without further a due, how about we get started on those Seven steps.

Step #1:
Make A Decision.

Definition of "Decision": "A conclusion or resolution reached after consideration. To break off, start a new, to start fresh." This is the easiest part, but unfortunately the hardest step because it is the first. Step one will not work if you're just "annoyed" at your situation. You must desire a fresh start and be willing to fight for it. You must want something new, that you can taste it. You must be at a point where enough is enough, that where you are in life is completely unacceptable and to continue living another day that way is disrespect to your name. You must know and believe that you are better than your circumstance, that you are better than your current situation, and then you must decide to become that more. Only then will you be ready for the next six steps.

Step #2:
Change Your Surroundings.

The smartest thing that I did when I was homeless was, I didn't hang around other people who were homeless because I knew that if I did, that if I had learned where to get a hot meal on a Sunday, a bed on a Saturday, and clothing on a Friday, if I had learned the system and gosh forbid made a friend, that I would still be homeless today. I would have remained homeless. No matter what situation you are in, you should know that if you're going to changing anything, you must first change the ones that you "hang around with" the most.

This could be tough at first because sometimes the ones we "hang around with the most" are exactly the ones that are holding us back. These are usually those who say that they "know us the best." Point blank, if they are not helping you get out of your current situation, then they are hurting you and keeping you in your current situation longer. You must have the courage to leave them. Even if that person or person(s) are you very own family members. Remember, birds of a feather flock together. If you truly want to change your life then you must break away from the flock. You can always come back to them after you've changed your situation and after you've become the newer and more improved you. If you're homeless, move to another part of the city where there aren't so many other homeless people. Try to wash up in public bathrooms the best that you can, and change your clothes often by checking dumpsters at second hand clothing stores. They usually throw out slightly used clothing that can't be sold in their stores because of stains or slight tears. That's gold to you. Interact and smile with as many people as you can that have everything. Even if they don't smile or interact back, be around those who have *everything*. This is important because just being around them will give you hope that one day you too will have everything again. I used to hang around a 7-11 and say 'hi' to everyone that I caught eye contact.

It gave me amazing hope that one day I would look like them and speak like them again. This will help you change your mindset, get you 'out of your funk', and improve your current situation fast.

Step #3:
Know That You're Alone in This and That's a Good Thing.

When I called my mom, and told her that I was homeless, instead of her saying that she would pay for my plane ticket home, make me a bowl of soup, and let me sleep in my old bed...instead of her saying that, she said "Why don't you just go to a shelter." I look back on it now and realize that my Mom did exactly what she was supposed to do, but at that point, I knew that I was in this all by myself. I had to realize that I got myself into this mess and that I had to be responsible for getting myself out of it. Stop waiting for someone to save you from you. No one is coming to save you until you decide to save yourself first. There is no Prince Charming that is going to ride in on a white steed to whisk you away from your problems.

No one is going to turn the corner, see you sleeping on the curb, and give you the keys to their house, car, and business. They are not going to change your life for you just because you're a nice person or because you know who to blame in your 'It wasn't my fault' story. You must realize that this is *your* journey and only *you* can save you from *you*. Without blaming anyone and this is a good thing, because once you realize no one is coming to save you, you take responsibility for where you are at, and you start to make amazingly clear decisions from that point on what you need to do to get yourself out of your situation. Right now. Once you do this,

once you have made a decision, you change your surroundings, and take responsibility, the universe immediately starts to move mountains on your behalf and you begin to see some incredible things start to open up in your life.

Step #4:
When there is no evidence, just Believe.

Definition of "Belief": "To accept something as true, genuine, or real." It costs nothing for you to believe in something. It's priceless to believe in yourself. Now that you've realized that you're in this alone, and that you must take responsibility for where you are and for where you want to be, you now have a great starting point to make some real tangible life changes. You must first believe deep down inside you that nothing is going to stop you from getting out of your situation and getting what you want out of life. That you are more powerful than you think and that you can and will make it out successful. You must believe this so whole-heartedly that no matter what anyone tells you, that you will not be deterred.

With belief comes a clear vision in yourself, of what you want and how to get it. This point in change is very powerful. Once you have a clear vision of yourself living debt free, living without addiction, living without that abusive spouse, and even better, no longer living homeless, draw up a plan—I like to call them destinations—complete with actionable steps that you will take to get what you want, now. Once you have those destinations don't be afraid to ask for help. Even if it means turning to those who might not know you and letting them know that you need help to get yourself to a better place. Share your destinations with them and you will be surprised who will give you a hand up once you've decided to save yourself.

Step #5:
Take Action Now.

Definition of "Taking Action": "An act of one that may be characterized by physical or mental movement." Let's look back on everything you've learned so far. You have belief, you've asked for help, and found someone who will give you a leg up. You've created clear 'destinations' of where you are now and where you want to be. You've realized that you have gotten yourself in this mess and that you are the only one who can get yourself out of it. You've changed your surroundings and you've made a decision. Now, you've been working out your brain muscle up to this point, and now it's time to work out your legs, arms and back muscles. You are now ready to do 'the work.' Believe it or not, this is where the fun begins, because now you get to see everything change not just your mental state, but your physical world as well. Notice that the definition of "taking action" means to act in both the physical and mental for movement. Every morning when I wake up I do 120 push-ups, but could you believe that there was a time when I couldn't even do one? I woke up one morning and decided that I would do one pushup, and I did. The next day, I woke up and I decided to do two, and I did two. The following week I was doing ten push-ups a day, and the following month I was up to sixty push-ups per day. That is how progress works. Don't try to do everything in one day or overnight. Instead, act and do one thing, tomorrow do two things, and the day after do three things. Do above what you did yesterday and that will help you. Everyday strive to do one better than yesterday, and before you know it you would have met your 'destination' without trying to do twenty things all at the same time. And that leads us to number six.

Step #6:
Stay Fucking Persistent.

The definition of "To Persist": "To continue steadfastly or firmly in some state, purpose, course of action or direction despite opposition." I love the last few words of the definition because the definition itself tells us immediately that we are going to come across pitfalls. How awesome is that? After reading the definition you shouldn't be surprised when you come across opportunities to grow even more. It says so right there in the definition. Yeah, you're going to have your opposition (I like to call them hurdles), but if you stay steadfast, and continue to walk your path, and continue to make the changes that you need to make, you will not only become the person you've always wanted to become, but you'll also enjoy the journey that much more because of what it took to get there. Your mind is everything. Wherever the mind goes, the body will follow. Keep believing in you and your body will get you there. Stay persistent.

Step #7:
Know That You Are Better Than This.

You've got what it takes, but it will take everything you've got. Sit back, relax, and put your life on cruise control because now you are on your way! You've overcome hurdles, you've stayed persistent, you've acted, you're seeing your destinations come to reality right in front of our own eyes and you have the utmost belief in yourself that are going to get where you are going. There is no doubt if you will or will not get there, the only question is when. You've got that part of your life locked down, so congratulations to you! You are amazing. I am so proud of you, but that doesn't mean that you can settle. Your job (if you choose to accept it) is to do more, be more and enjoy more. Never think that where you are right now is good enough, because true bliss could be just around the next corner. Speaking of true bliss, now that your mental and physical game is on point, you now must approach your spiritual game. See, you cannot align your mind, body, and soul if one is nonexistent or slacking. Now it is time for you to dig deep down, to align your mind, body, and soul with your destinations. You must make the decision that you will forgive those who weren't there for you, in the beginning of your journey and in life.

You must if you want to enjoy all of your future successes. Spiritually, as well. For me, it meant calling my mom and telling her that I forgave her for telling me to go to a shelter when I called her begging for help at the lowest point of my life. I didn't just forgive her for not helping me, I forgave her for everything and anything that she might have done to hurt my feelings. Those that I remembered when I was six years old and those that I had forgotten about later in life. I forgave her completely and you will have to do the same.

You might not have a mother, father, sibling or a friend to forgive, but you will have to forgive that one person (if not more) who was not there for you when you needed them the most. This might even include forgiving you for you. Don't get me wrong, you're not forgiving them for them. You're forgiving them for you. To truly take your life to the next level, you must be able to heal, close that old door and persist with a smile on your face in the direction of these new doors that are now opening. Knowing that you have the power to forgive someone is astounding, and once you've truly forgiven someone, almost immediately after, you will feel like a new person. Continue to work hard, love hard, never settle, forgive and go farther. Your life is only going to get that much more exciting and amazing from this point on! You'll see! Never settle. Forgive. Go farther and jump towards the stars! Because you're worth it.

Receive More:

Steps and strategies.

Want more 'Tips?' Get them and more emailed to your inbox. Visit www.WeWin360.com and subscribe to one of our paid email communities.

BONUS CHAPTER
I still love cookies

NEWLY ADDED CHAPTER
I still love cookies

FIRST AND FOREMOST, thank you so much for purchasing my book and taking the time out of your day to read it, to like it online, and share it with your friends and family. My goal with telling my story is to remind you that no matter how old or how young you are, that you can absolutely have everything and anything you want in this world. I hope that I've inspired you, no matter where you are now in life. I hope that my story gives you the motivation to kick start that raging fire I know you have deep down inside you and I hope that you will use it to make the critical life changes you need to make, to live your life with plenty of fulfillment. Oh! And by the way, I still love cookies.

I also hope that my story restores your faith in humanity and gives you the fuel that you need to go out there and change the world. Even if it's just one random act of kindness at a time.

Where am I now?

Today as you read this it's been just over a few years since I've been homeless, and I can absolutely say that I am in love with my life. I broke up with myself (see more of what I mean by this by visiting www.WeWin360.com) and of course, I'm no longer homeless. So, don't worry about where to send me food in the mail, I'm alive and eating food that isn't found in a garbage can anymore. I'm eating quite well today, healthy, and I'm preparing my own food in my own kitchen, imagine that! I currently live in a beautiful house in Las Vegas. It was recently built, and it's in a gated community surrounded by families with young children, parks and bike trails. From where I have been it's true bliss. I rent with a roommate, so I don't own it, but you know, I'm getting one step closer every day.

A couple months after getting back on my feet and starting that new job where I was hired to sell mobile apps to business owners I started a community volunteer program right here in Las Vegas focused on benefiting those who we call 'Less fortunate.' Less fortunate to us is anyone who is unemployed, under employed, and or homeless. People like to call it 'Philanthropy', I just call it 'Doing the right thing.' I started our organization with a single pot of spaghetti. I went down into the homeless corridor with my single pot of spaghetti and served Thirty people. The following Monday I went back with two pots of spaghetti and served sixty people. Then I went home and told somebody what I did and the following Monday they came back with me. Then they went home and told somebody what we both did and they brought somebody back with them. And we just started to grow and grow.

Fast forward just a few years and now we have an organization that has over one hundred full time volunteers and we serve anywhere from 250 to 560 less fortunate people every week. This doesn't include any of our holiday events where we serve. This is just our weekly commitment.

All the food that we serve comes from our own personal kitchens and all the clothing that we hand out comes from our own personal closets. We serve them with fresh food, clothing, hygiene, hugs, and love all for free.

We also provide tools for those who are less fortunate that are looking to get back on to their feet by being a bridge to providing access to other organizations that help with obtaining I.D.'s, job training, job placement, temporary housing and birth certificates.

I sit on the board of two non-profits, I've spoken on the panel as a guest speaker at non-profit expos and conventions. We also teamed up with HUD and started a food rescue program (HUD is The United States Department of Housing and Urban Development.) We together rescue food that is otherwise unsold from local grocery stores and we deliver that same food, in the same hour, for free to families who have a roof over their heads, but can't afford that food for free. This program helps us serve and additional 700 individual meals per week all for free.

As far as my son, I do have him back in my life and I help pay for his daycare and anything else that he needs. He unfortunately no longer lives in Las Vegas or in Nevada, but he's still close. About an hour flight from Las Vegas one way. He's surrounded by family on his mom's side, cousins, corn fields and greenery. His mom decided it was best to move back to where she had grown up so that he could be around her family. I talk to him sometimes twice a week and every Sunday. I visited him just recently and plan to visit him again on my birthday.

Regarding my ex, we are fantastic! I know now that there is no better person in the world, if not myself, that can raise him the way he needs to be raised than her. I know that I've put her through a lot, mentally and emotionally, and for that I will be forever sorry. I am also grateful for her because she is a great mom to him. She's moved on, she's currently dating someone new and I could not be any happier for her! I don't know him, but if he treats my son with the same amount of respect he treats her, he'll always be okay in my book.

Me? Well, I'm single.

I haven't found my new yet and to be honest, I don't need to. I'm sure that when the universe sees fit that the right person will walk into my life ready to complete me. For now, it's all about my continual personal growth and personal transformation. Getting to the next stage in my awesomeness.

This is what I've learned so far…

I know today that I would have never made it through and out of my experience if it wasn't for GOD. He is truly my Lord and savior. I know this because, I cannot tell you why my cell phone stayed on the entire time when I was homeless even though I hadn't paid the bill in seven months. I can't tell you why Eric was there every time I needed him. I can't tell you why I was able to talk rideshares into giving me rides to work when I didn't have a single dime in my pocket or why my roommate (of the first place I lived in after going homeless) allowed me to move in without any money for rent or a deposit. The only thing that I can tell you is that once I made a conscience decision to never eat out of another garbage can and once I made the conscience decision to trust in him, that everything "supernaturally" started to fall in place. I still had to believe and work my ass off, but it worked, he worked. Now I don't know if you are a religious person or if you believe in the Universe, Buddha or your pet goldfish, all I can truly tell you is that if you believe in anything much bigger than yourself and are willing to do the work, you can have anything you want in the world.

I've also learned that you must embrace your failures because your failures are part of who you are. Your failure makes you stronger, your failures make you aware of what you need to do to get more out of life. Even though as a society we tend to poke fun at those who fail, and glorify those who've succeeded, we need to understand that even those who have succeeded have also failed, a lot. Most likely a numerous amount of times before they found a way to succeed at what they are succeeding at today. At one point in my life I was ashamed to tell my story. I felt ashamed, embarrassed, alone and of course, like a failure. Today, I speak my story to others to give them the direction of what they want because I've realized that journeys have power. With stories you can inspire, you can relate, you can motivate and if all your intentions are good, you can be the light that shines in the lives of those who are lost in the dark.

If I could leave you with anything I leave you with this, embrace your inner you and don't be afraid to tell your story, ever. You never know whose life you will change by announcing to the world that you are 'BETTER THAN THIS!'

www.BetterThanThisTheBook.com

Inspired?

See what M. Holis is up to now!

Visit www.WeWin360.com and see what he's been up to.

"I'm not trying to change the world,
I'm just creating one that matches my vision for it."
M. Holis

ABOUT THE AUTHOR

Purpose powered

ABOUT THE AUTHOR

Purpose powered

VOTED TOP 100 MEN OF THE YEAR IN LAS VEGAS. AWARDED BY THE UNITED STATES CONGRESS & SENATE FOR LEADERSHIP IN PHILANTHROPY.

M. Holis believes that no one person should ever go hungry. Not for food or for knowledge.

Since getting back on his feet he has been called a philanthropist, crusader for the homeless, humanitarian, and leader in the community he practices the act of radical generosity that transforms the world. As the founder of the grassroots organization that gives, he lives to radically change the world by serving those who are less fortunate, underemployed, and unemployed with food, clothing, hygiene, hugs, love all for free.

After getting back on his feet just a few years ago, he decided to create a 100% community-based organization of volunteers that, to date, has had over 5,435 locals come down and pay it forward with them, now has over 105 volunteers and has given out over 91,438 individual meals, locally, all for free. Completely nondenominational and independent of any major charity or church. They're just people serving people.

His community projects have included the likes of, Rich Products, Starbucks, Einstein Bagels, Coca-Cola and more.

As a leader in philanthropy his organization has been **Awarded Certificate of Special Congressional Recognition by The United States Congress** for an unwavering commitment and leadership to help the disadvantaged people of Las Vegas. They've been **Awarded Senatorial Recognition by The United States Senate.** Given by, Senator Dean Heller.
- *Awarded Las Vegas* ***Top 100 Men of the year*** *and Awarded hometown hero.*

His newest project; www.WeWin360.com, is a three-day workshop for 'Givers' who are looking to take their giving to the next level. By creating effective and exceptional volunteer organizations. Whether in life, in businesses, or in community.

Inspired to take your 'Giving game' to the next level? Visit www.WeWin360.com and join us at our next three-day workshop. Exclusively for non-profits, grassroots organizations, and volunteers. Join us

I want to hear from you

How has my book inspired you?

Leave your testimonial on Amazon

Follow me on Facebook

Friend me on Linkedin

Join our tribe of givers at

www.WeWin360.com

MY DEDICATIONS

Who this book is dedicated to

MY DEDICATIONS
Who this book is dedicated to

FIRST AND FOREMOST, THIS BOOK IS DEDICATED TO MY SON AND HIS VERY LOVING MOTHER.

This book is also dedicated to her family for taking care of him in times when I could not. To Jonathan, Eric, Tori M. (the first person on the planet to ever know my story), to David who, after I told him my story, told me to never tell my story to anyone, ever again. To my roommate after going homelessness, and to my old boss for giving me that old commission check that nearly saved my life. To Christine for the poem, thank you! To Eryn Mills at Eonsmills.com for your tireless editing efforts. For taking what was a pitiful excuse for literature (my original journal) and spending hours editing it down to what we have created today (The book that you hold in your hands.) To Steelhead Productions "Exhibit Happy" for sponsoring our first printed edition of my book. To every single volunteer, team navigator, every single newbie that has come down to our Monday night servings to help us serve those who are less fortunate every single Monday. To Father John and to every corporate sponsor that has helped us serve over ninety-one thousand meals individually, locally (independent of any major charity organization) in our community for free.

To my publisher (Who's brother company) also publishes Dr. Wayne Dyer and Oprah's books, thank you for believing in Me and in my journal (before it became this book.) Who, believe it or not, also continues to believe in the books that I have yet to write. 'Better Than This' Part Two?

To my immediate family, to my sister (I love you dearly), my brothers, my nephews, to my uncles (alive and passed), to my grandfather who is the biggest inspiration in my life still to this day (recently passed), to my grandmother who is very much alive and kicking today who reminds me every day that 'Ain't is not a word', and to my mom for her support and her incredible tough love.

To our entire staff and crew at WeWin360.com for your tireless efforts in a making sure that every workshop that we produce provides exceptional results for every student who attends.

To every single person who is currently less fortunate and received this book as part of our pay if forward book program, this book is for you. Stay strong, go left when others go right, remember your seven steps, remember to never, ever, ever give up and remember, "Just because you're eating out of garbage cans, doesn't mean that you are garbage."

YOU ARE...
Better Than This

For more about our 'Buy a book, Give a book' pay it forward (bulk book buying) program of 100 books or more, email:

ImBetterThanThisTheBook@gmail.com

Every book purchased through our buy a book (bulk buy) program provides a book to someone who can't afford one, locally. Your books will be distributed among our local less fortunate. Those who we call 'Future Friends.'

For wholesale orders email us at:

ImBetterThanThisTheBook@gmail.com

Hire M. Holis to tell his story at your next event.
Email: ImBetterThanThisTheBook@gmail.com
ATT: Speaking Events Coordinator!

BETTER THAN THIS

Part 2 (Coming soon)

Printed in the United States
By Bookmasters